THE ULTIMATE BOOK OF DINOSAURS

Claudia Martin

Consultant: Dougal Dixon

ARCTURUS

ARCTURUS

This edition published in 2021 by Arcturus Publishing Limited
26/27 Bickels Yard, 151–153 Bermondsey Street,
London SE1 3HA

Copyright © Arcturus Holdings Limited

ISBN: 978-1-83940-598-3
CH007797NT
Supplier 26, Date 0221, Print run 10469

Printed in China

Author: Claudia Martin
Designer: Lorraine Inglis
Primary Illustrator: Mat Edwards
Consultant: Dougal Dixon
Editor: Rebecca Clunes
Art Direction: Rosie Bellwood
Editorial Manager: Joe Harris

In this book, one billion means one thousand million (1,000,000,000) and one trillion means one million million (1,000,000,000,000).

THE ULTIMATE BOOK OF
DINOSAURS

CONTENTS

THE DAYS OF DINOSAURS

Dinosaurs first walked the Earth around 233 million years ago. For the next 167 million years, dinosaurs were the fiercest and largest animals on every continent. Millions of gentle plant-eating dinosaurs also roamed across swamps, forests, and deserts, defending themselves against their dangerous relatives with their speed, immense size, or sharp horns.

The dinosaurs were reptiles, like today's scaly-skinned lizards and crocodiles. Like most reptiles, female dinosaurs laid eggs. Some dinosaurs walked on four legs and others on two, but they all had four limbs. The key difference between dinosaurs and other reptiles was that dinosaurs walked with their back legs held straight under their body rather than sprawled to the sides. This made them faster and able to grow bigger and heavier. Although some dinosaurs strode into rivers and lakes to snatch prey, they were land-living animals.

There were around 1,000 different species of dinosaurs. Each member of a species looked similar and behaved in a similar way. The earliest dinosaur species were small meat-eaters. Yet over millions of years, dinosaurs changed their habits and appearance, growing larger or smaller, starting to eat plants, or even developing wings. While new species developed, others died out after a few million years. Species ranged from tiny, quick dinosaurs such as *Parvicursor*, just 39 cm (15 in) long, to the slow-moving plant-eater *Argentinosaurus*, up to 39.7 m (139 ft) long. Around 66 million years ago, a massive asteroid plummeted into Earth. Every dinosaur species was wiped out by the disaster, apart from some that had developed wings and earned themselves a new name: birds.

Kosmoceratops was a species of plant-eating dinosaur that lived in North America from 76 to 75 million years ago. It was 4.5 m (15 ft) long and weighed about as much as a hippo.

In Asia, around 67 million years ago, the long-jawed meat-eater *Qianzhousaurus* tries to catch a feathered, winged dinosaur called *Nankangia*.

Birth of the Earth

Around 4.5 billion years ago, Earth formed in a cloud of gas and dust that was spinning around the young Sun. Tiny, simple living things appeared in Earth's oceans around 3.5 billion years ago. It was only 0.23 billion years ago that the first dinosaurs walked the Earth.

Along with the other planets in the Solar System, Earth was born in the gas and dust left over from the formation of the Sun. Gravity began to pull the gas and dust into clumps. The third large clump from the Sun became Earth. As the material crashed together, it gave out an enormous amount of heat, warming the new Earth to around 5,000°C (9,000°F).

Heavy metals, mostly iron and nickel, sank to form the core of our planet, around 6,970 km (4,330 miles) across. Lighter materials moved toward the surface, forming molten rock.

For the first 500 million years, Earth was baking hot and surrounded by poisonous gases. Slowly, Earth cooled enough for its outer layer of rock to harden. Water started to cover much of Earth's surface, forming oceans, while the atmosphere we breathe today took shape. Now the conditions were right for life to thrive.

The dinosaur *Liliensternus* lived around 0.23 billion years ago, around 3.27 billion years after the first living things evolved.

Evolution

As Earth itself has changed, so have the animals and plants that live on it. Over millions of years, living things change, or evolve, developing new features that help them survive. Natural disasters, causing sudden changes in temperature or sea level, can also drive some living things to extinction.

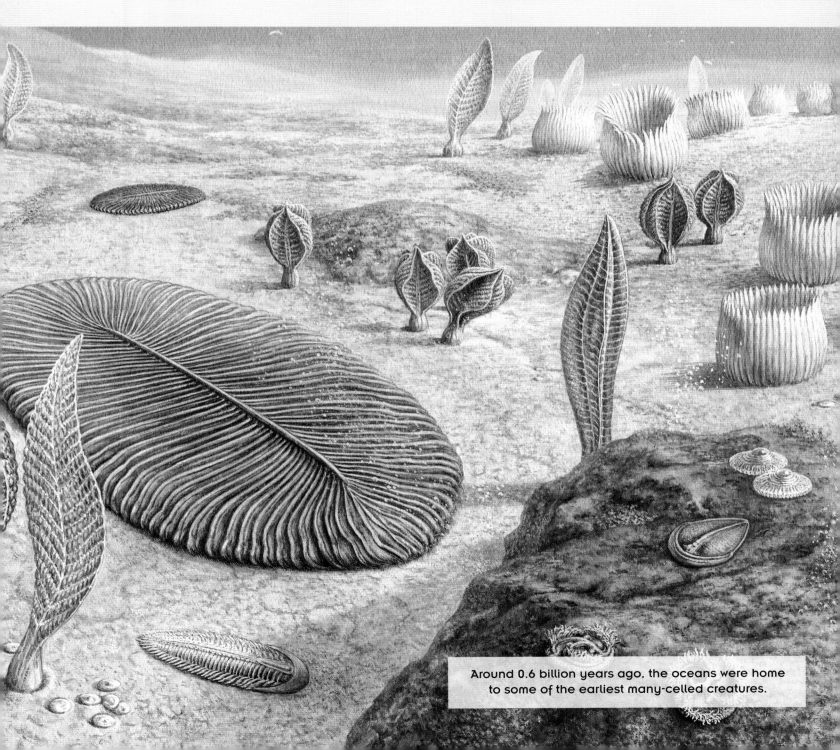

All living things evolved from life forms called archaea, which are just one tiny, simple cell. Dinosaurs were made of trillions of cells.

Around 0.6 billion years ago, the oceans were home to some of the earliest many-celled creatures.

CHANGING PLANET

Earth has not always looked as it does today. Over the last 4.5 billion years, the shapes of the continents, the climate, and the depth of the oceans have been through constant, but extremely slow, changes. Many of these changes have been caused by the movement of the plates of rock that form Earth's surface.

Scientists divide the history of Earth into periods of time called—from longest to shortest—eons (or aeons), eras, periods, and epochs. The beginnings and ends of these time periods are marked by major events, such as big steps forward in evolution or catastrophes that caused widespread extinctions. Scientists have learned about these events by studying rocks and fossils. The dinosaurs evolved during the Triassic Period, began to dominate the land during the Jurassic Period, and died out at the end of the Cretaceous Period.

The Earth's surface is formed by giant plates of solid rock, called tectonic plates, which fit together a little like jigsaw pieces. Over time, the flow of hot rock beneath these plates has moved them across Earth's surface. This has changed the shapes of continents, as well as pushed up mountains and caused volcanoes and earthquakes where the edges of plates press into each other. Large volcanic eruptions can change Earth's climate, making the air warmer or cooler and lowering or raising the level of the sea.

A high number of volcanic eruptions released lots of carbon dioxide gas, which traps heat around Earth.

Triassic Period: 252–201 million years ago

Pangea

Movement of Earth's plates had formed one landmass, a supercontinent called Pangea.

The climate was so warm there was no ice at the Poles.

Jurassic Period: 201–145 million years ago

Laurasia

Gondwana

Pangea had split in two, creating two main landmasses.

Cretaceous Period: 145–66 million years ago

North America
Europe
Asia
Africa
South America
Australia
Antarctica

As the landmasses broke into smaller regions, dinosaurs evolved to have greater differences in different environments.

Today

North America
Europe
Asia
Africa
South America
Australia
Antarctica

For the last 5 million years, the continents have looked much as they do today.

Cretaceous swamp

During the warm Cretaceous Period, shallow seas covered much of the continents.

Around 450 million years ago, a shelled, 5.5-m (18-ft) long *Endoceras* hunts among the jawless fish *Promissum* and *Sacabambaspis*, while the invertebrate *Isotelus* scuttles over the seafloor.

LIFE BEGINS

Life began in the oceans and remained there for around 2 billion years. During this time, life forms evolved from single-celled archaea to many-celled animals and plants. Eventually, some animals developed backbones, becoming the first vertebrates. Later still, some vertebrates grew four legs, making them the ancestors of dinosaurs—and humans.

The earliest living things were not animals: they were tiny, basic life forms called microorganisms. The earliest known animals evolved around 665 million years ago. Animals can move, eat other living things, and need oxygen to survive. The earliest animals were soft bodied, without shells or backbones. They absorbed oxygen from the water. These animals were the ancestors of today's invertebrates (animals without backbones), such as jellyfish.

Around 540 million years ago, some animals started to grow shells. These may have been useful for protection or for weighting down the animal so it did not drift in the current. Some of these early shelled creatures were the ancestors of today's snails and crabs.

The earliest vertebrates evolved around 520 million years ago. These fish-like creatures sucked up food rather than biting it, as they did not have jaws. After another 60 million years, the first animals with jaws evolved. Among them were shark-like fish. The first four-legged animals, known as tetrapods, evolved from bony fish around 367 million years ago.

Ammonites, which were invertebrates with spiral shells, lived in the oceans between 240 and 66 million years ago.

Tetrapods

Early tetrapods lived mostly in shallow water, but their four legs enabled them to walk on land. Like their fish ancestors, they had body parts called gills for taking oxygen from the water. However, they had also evolved lungs for breathing air. Amphibians were among the earliest tetrapods. Modern amphibians include frogs and salamanders, which lay eggs in water and usually spend part of their life in water and part on land. Later tetrapods—the reptiles, birds, and mammals—no longer had gills, relying on lungs alone to breathe air. Unlike their reptile ancestors, mammals also developed hair and started to feed their babies on milk.

Living around 365 million years ago, *Acanthostega* was one of the earliest known tetrapods. Its four legs were used for both swimming and walking in shallow swamps.

FOSSILS

Without fossils, we would not know that dinosaurs and other extinct animals had ever existed. Fossils are the preserved remains of an animal or plant that lived thousands, millions, or even billions of years ago. Sometimes the animal's body has been preserved in rock. At other times, we find an animal-shaped hole, footprint, or burrow.

When an animal dies, its body usually rots. However, a fossil can form if the body is quickly covered with sand or mud. Even then, the animal's soft parts, such as flesh, muscles, and feathers, usually rot, leaving behind the bones, teeth, and shells. Very slowly, the sand or mud around the body hardens into rock. Water seeps into the bones, teeth, and shells, dissolving them. Yet minerals in the water fill the space left behind, creating a rock copy. Footprints and burrows can be fossilized if they are baked hard by the sun, then covered by sand and mud. Occasionally, a fossil forms without the animal being turned into rock, when the whole body is preserved in ice, tar, or sticky tree resin.

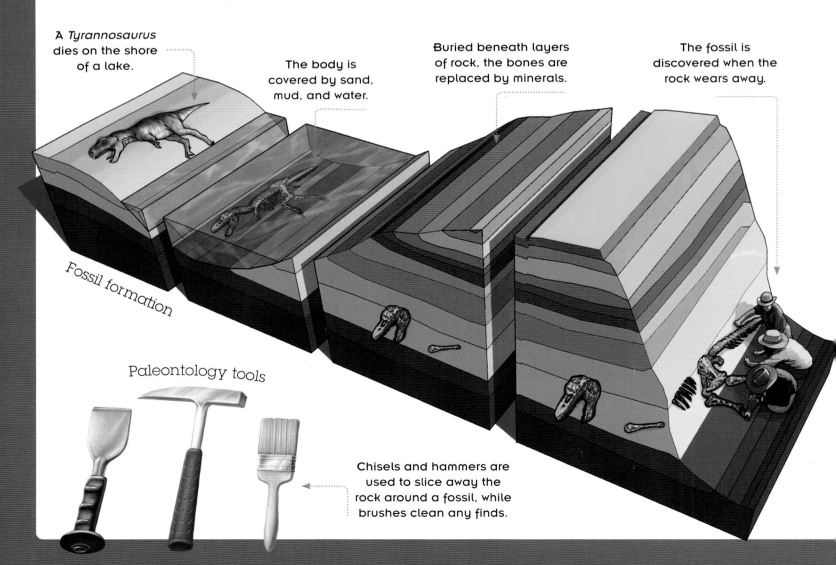

A *Tyrannosaurus* dies on the shore of a lake.

The body is covered by sand, mud, and water.

Buried beneath layers of rock, the bones are replaced by minerals.

The fossil is discovered when the rock wears away.

Fossil formation

Paleontology tools

Chisels and hammers are used to slice away the rock around a fossil, while brushes clean any finds.

Scientists who study fossils are called paleontologists. They carefully uncover fossils, then piece together how a dinosaur may have looked by examining the shapes of the bones, as well as any marks on the bones where muscles were once attached. By studying the layers of rock where a fossil was found, they work out how long ago the dinosaur lived.

The tooth of a mosasaur, an extinct swimming reptile, has been turned to rock.

Trace fossil

Body fossil

This theropod dinosaur footprint is known as a trace fossil because it is the trace of a long-dead animal rather than the animal itself.

Mold (or mould) and cast fossils

As this plant was pressed under sand, minerals in its leaves left behind a print on the sandstone rock.

Compression fossil

Some of these fossils of ammonites are called molds (or moulds), because the shape of the shell has been left behind as rock hardened around it. Others are casts, where the inside of the shell filled with minerals.

EARLY REPTILES

Reptiles evolved from amphibians around 312 million years ago.
They were the first vertebrates to spend all their time on land.
Unlike amphibians, which lay soft eggs that must be kept damp,
reptiles usually lay hard-shelled eggs on land. The shell stops
the baby drying out. The earliest reptiles had simple skulls,
but some later reptiles developed lighter, more complex skulls.

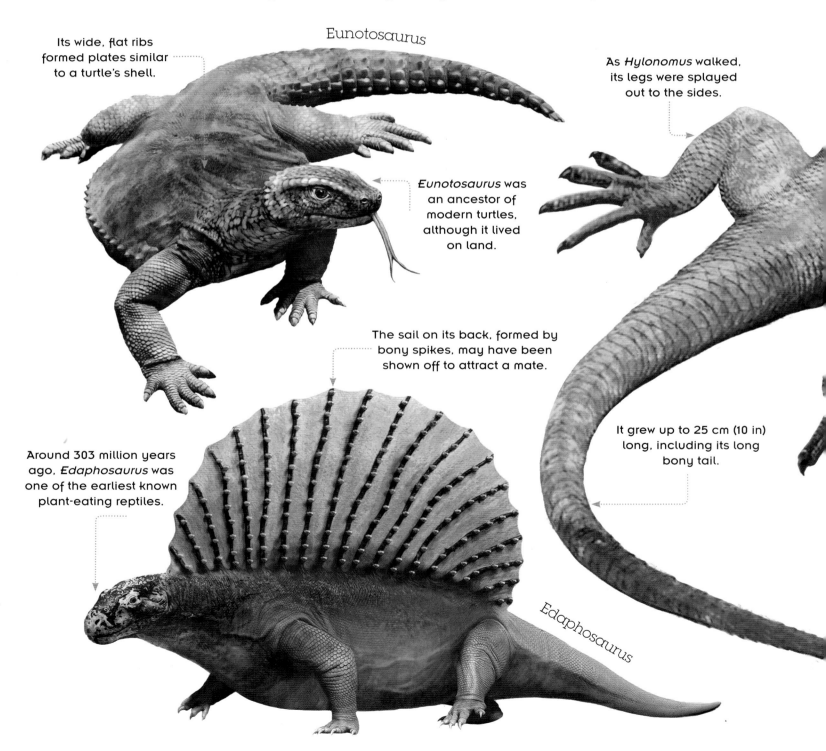

Eunotosaurus

Its wide, flat ribs formed plates similar to a turtle's shell.

As *Hylonomus* walked, its legs were splayed out to the sides.

Eunotosaurus was an ancestor of modern turtles, although it lived on land.

The sail on its back, formed by bony spikes, may have been shown off to attract a mate.

It grew up to 25 cm (10 in) long, including its long bony tail.

Around 303 million years ago, *Edaphosaurus* was one of the earliest known plant-eating reptiles.

Edaphosaurus

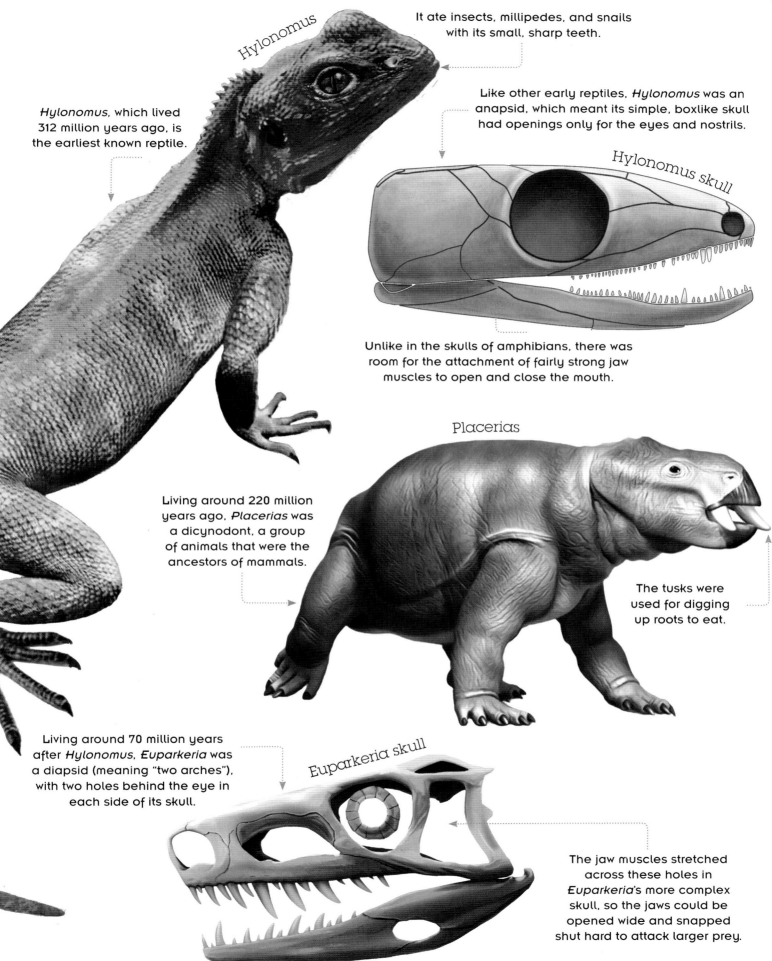

Hylonomus

It ate insects, millipedes, and snails with its small, sharp teeth.

Hylonomus, which lived 312 million years ago, is the earliest known reptile.

Like other early reptiles, *Hylonomus* was an anapsid, which meant its simple, boxlike skull had openings only for the eyes and nostrils.

Hylonomus skull

Unlike in the skulls of amphibians, there was room for the attachment of fairly strong jaw muscles to open and close the mouth.

Placerias

Living around 220 million years ago, *Placerias* was a dicynodont, a group of animals that were the ancestors of mammals.

The tusks were used for digging up roots to eat.

Living around 70 million years after *Hylonomus*, *Euparkeria* was a diapsid (meaning "two arches"), with two holes behind the eye in each side of its skull.

Euparkeria skull

The jaw muscles stretched across these holes in *Euparkeria*'s more complex skull, so the jaws could be opened wide and snapped shut hard to attack larger prey.

First Dinosaurs

Around 233 million years ago, dinosaurs evolved from a group of diapsid reptiles. Like later dinosaurs, the earliest dinosaurs lived on land. They walked on their two back legs, grasping little animals with their hands. Most early dinosaurs were small—far smaller than the giant dinosaurs that would evolve over the next 167 million years.

The diapsid reptiles, which evolved around 307 million years ago, had lightweight skulls with strong jaws. Most modern reptiles, including lizards, snakes, and crocodiles, are diapsids. Turtles are the only living reptiles with a simpler anapsid skull.

Around 250 million years ago, the diapsids split into two main groups: the archosaurs, or "ruling reptiles," and the lepidosaurs. The early lepidosaurs were the ancestors of today's snakes and lizards, while the early archosaurs were the ancestors of dinosaurs, crocodiles, and pterosaurs, which were flying reptiles. Archosaurs had an advantage over other reptiles: their teeth were set deep into sockets, making them less likely to be torn out during feeding. They also had extra openings in their skulls, making them even more lightweight.

The dinosaurs evolved an additional advantage over other archosaurs: they walked with their back legs held straight beneath their body rather than sprawled to the sides, so the legs could carry more weight and take longer strides. All these advantages led to the dinosaurs becoming the most successful and widespread land animals for many millions of years.

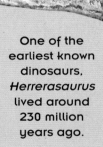

One of the earliest known dinosaurs, *Herrerasaurus* lived around 230 million years ago.

Dinosaur Stance

The hips and legs of dinosaurs had evolved to give a more upright stance than that of other reptiles, including modern lizards. Although lizards can run fast, their body has to wriggle from side to side as they swing their legs forward, pressing on first the left lung and then the right lung. This is why lizards have to stop to catch their breath after running, even when at risk of attack. The upright stance of dinosaurs enabled them to breathe easily while running. In addition, their straight back legs carried their weight straight to the ground, so the back legs could take all their body weight, freeing up their front limbs for grabbing prey.

Lizard stance

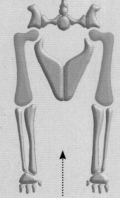

Dinosaur stance

A dinosaur's thigh bones, called femurs, were bent at right angles at the top.

Around 1 m (3.3 ft) long, the early dinosaur *Eoraptor* (right) chases a lizard through Triassic Argentina.

DINOSAUR GROUPS

Paleontologists divide dinosaurs into groups based on similarities between their skeletons, teeth, and bony plates. Similar dinosaurs are placed in the same species. Where species share key characteristics, they are grouped into a family, then larger groups such as classes. *Tyrannosaurus* is a species in the Tyrannosauridae family of large meat-eaters, in the archosaur class.

Paleontologists often divide dinosaurs into two major groups, called orders, based on their hip types: ornithischians and saurischians. The ornithischians, or "bird-hipped" dinosaurs, were plant-eaters. They were named for their hips' similarity to those of birds, but ornithischians were not closely related to birds, which actually evolved from saurischian dinosaurs. The saurischians, or "lizard-hipped" dinosaurs, included both meat-eaters and plant-eaters.

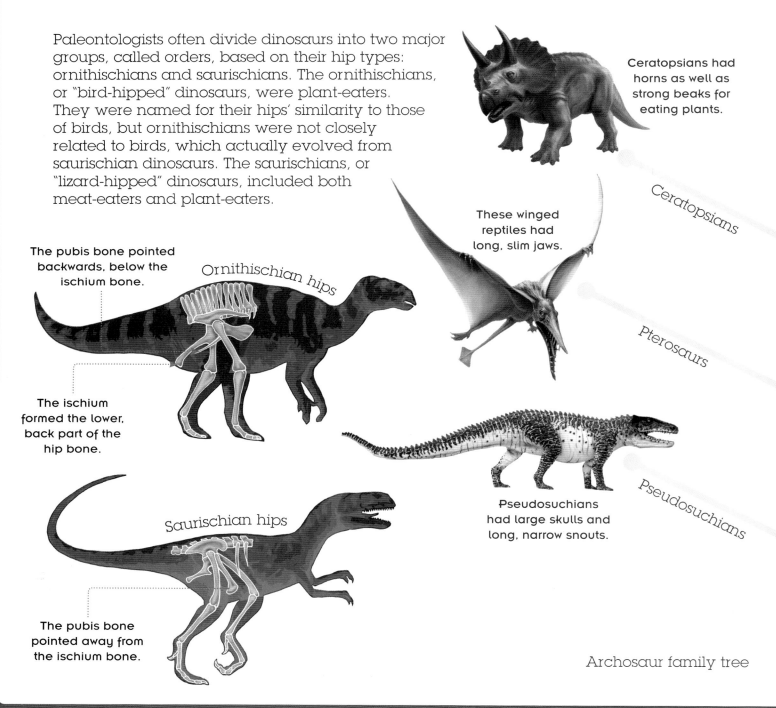

Ceratopsians had horns as well as strong beaks for eating plants.

Ceratopsians

These winged reptiles had long, slim jaws.

Pterosaurs

The pubis bone pointed backwards, below the ischium bone.

Ornithischian hips

The ischium formed the lower, back part of the hip bone.

Pseudosuchians had large skulls and long, narrow snouts.

Pseudosuchians

Saurischian hips

The pubis bone pointed away from the ischium bone.

Archosaur family tree

These plant-eaters had three-toed feet.

Sauropodomorphs were usually large, long-necked, long-tailed plant-eaters.

Plant-eating pachycephalosaurs had thick, often domed, skulls.

These plant-eaters had bodies protected by bony plates.

Most theropods were meat-eaters, with hollow bones and three-toed feet.

Pachycephalosaurs

Ornithopods

Thyreophorans

Sauropodomorphs

Cerapods

Theropods

Birds

Saurischians

Ornithischians

Dinosaurs

Birds evolved from a group of theropod dinosaurs around 130 million years ago.

The archosaur family tree includes pseudosuchians, the crocodile-like reptiles; pterosaurs, the flying reptiles; and dinosaurs. The pseudosuchians evolved before dinosaurs, around 250 million years ago. Pterosaurs evolved around the same time as dinosaurs, about 230 million years ago. The ornithischian dinosaurs were the cerapods, including ceratopsians, pachycephalosaurs, and ornithopods; and the thyreophorans. The saurischian dinosaurs were the sauropodomorphs and the theropods.

If they survived the impact, dinosaurs such as *Velafrons* died in the months following the asteroid's plunge into the shallow waters of the Gulf of Mexico.

END OF THE DINOSAURS

The dinosaurs died out around 66 million years ago. About three-quarters of all Earth's animal species became extinct alongside them. Scientists believe these catastrophic extinctions were the result of a large space rock, called an asteroid, crashing into Earth. The event marked the end of the Cretaceous Period.

Although scientists cannot be certain what caused the extinctions, they know that, around 66 million years ago, an asteroid crashed into the sea of the Gulf of Mexico, off the coast of North America. The asteroid, which was 10 to 15 km (6 to 9 miles) wide, was smashed in the impact. It left a crater 180 km (112 miles) wide.

The impact would have made tall waves flood the land. Fires would have been started by the heat of the explosion. The strike also sent immense clouds of dust into the air. These clouds would have blocked out the Sun's light and warmth for up to a year. This caused the deaths of many plants, which need sunlight to make their food. Without plants to eat, many plant-eaters would have died, followed by a lot of the meat-eaters that fed on them.

Very few tetrapods that weighed over 25 kg (55 lb) survived. Large animals, which need more food, very quickly could not find enough to eat. Animals that ate only meat or only plants also usually died. Some smaller animals survived if they ate seeds, insects, dead animals, or anything they could find. All the dinosaurs were wiped out, apart from some of those dinosaurs that had already evolved into birds (see pages 44–45).

Small mammals such as *Kimbetopsalis* survived the disaster, probably because their size enabled them to take shelter and find enough food.

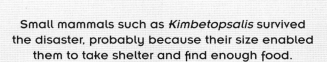

Death and Survival
Alongside the dinosaurs, the pterosaurs and many sea-living reptiles, including plesiosaurs and mosasaurs, died out. However, some reptiles did survive, including crocodiles, turtles, snakes, and lizards. Some fish, amphibians, mammals, and insects and other invertebrates also survived.

Many species of frogs, such as *Xenopus*, survived. Frogs grew much more widespread in the following years, moving into new habitats such as trees.

AFTER THE DINOSAURS

For the first few million years after the dinosaurs died, most of Earth's animals were small. Many of these survivors had been rare while dinosaurs walked the Earth and sharp-toothed reptiles swam in the seas. New animals now evolved to take the place of the dinosaurs, although they in turn became extinct over time. In particular, mammals stepped into the gap left by dinosaurs, becoming larger and more varied.

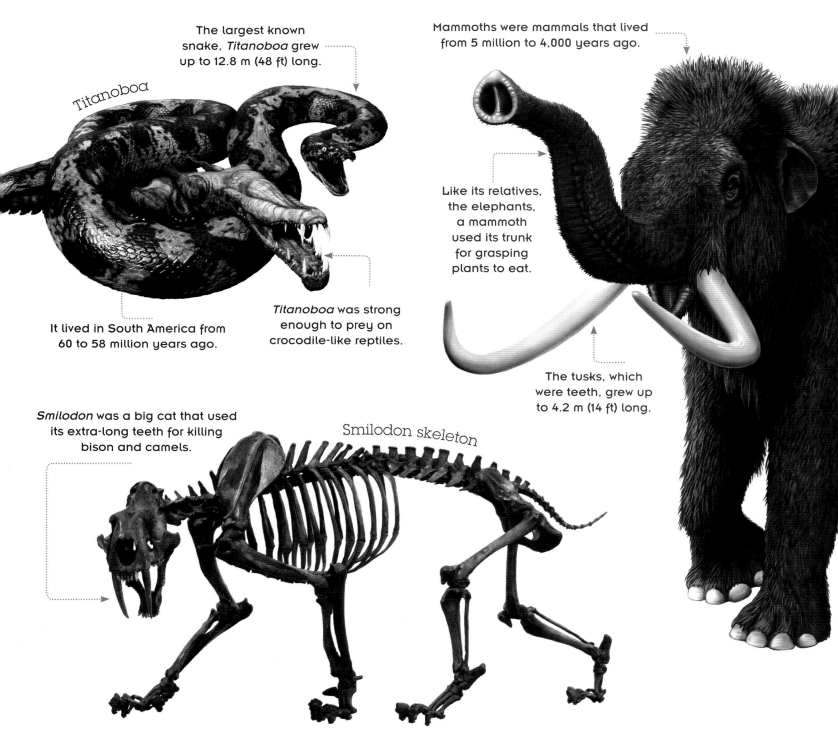

The largest known snake, *Titanoboa* grew up to 12.8 m (48 ft) long.

Titanoboa

Mammoths were mammals that lived from 5 million to 4,000 years ago.

Like its relatives, the elephants, a mammoth used its trunk for grasping plants to eat.

It lived in South America from 60 to 58 million years ago.

Titanoboa was strong enough to prey on crocodile-like reptiles.

The tusks, which were teeth, grew up to 4.2 m (14 ft) long.

Smilodon was a big cat that used its extra-long teeth for killing bison and camels.

Smilodon skeleton

Megalodon

Megalodon was the largest shark that ever lived, perhaps reaching 18 m (59 ft) long.

This extinct fish's sharp teeth were 18 cm (7.1 in) long.

Thick fur kept a mammoth warm during the last ice age, when Earth's temperature was much lower than today.

Woolly mammoth

This plant-eating sloth lived between 5 million and 12,000 years ago.

Megatherium was one of the largest known land mammals, reaching 6 m (20 ft) long.

Megatherium

Gastornis

The huge, hooked beak was probably used for cracking nuts and seeds.

This flightless bird grew to 2 m (6.6 ft) tall.

Like baby elephants, baby mammoths stayed close to their mother.

TIMELINE OF LIFE

Dinosaurs ruled the Earth for millions of years, but their time on our planet was only a small fraction of its long history. If the planet's 4.5 billion years are likened to a 24-hour day, the dinosaurs walked the Earth for less than an hour. Humans have been in existence for the last seven seconds of this "day."

Scientists do not know why the first simple living cells came into being in Earth's oceans. After this unexplained event, evolution moved very slowly for at least 1.5 billion years, before something almost as amazing happened: the first complex cells, called eukaryotes, developed. All animals and plants are made entirely of eukaryote cells.

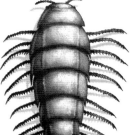

Euthycarcinus

Young Earth

Eukaryote

Dickinsonia

500 million years ago: Invertebrates may be the first animals to crawl on land.

4.5 billion years ago: The Earth forms from dust and gas.

2 billion years ago: Eukaryotes, which are cells with complex internal structures, evolve.

665 million years ago: The first animals, which are simple invertebrates, evolve.

| 5 | 4 | 3 | 2 | 1 | 0.6 | 0.5 |

Billion years ago
Dashes on the timeline represent a change in the scale.

3.5 billion years ago: The first archaea appear in the ocean.

900 million years ago: Living things made of more than one cell appear.

520 million years ago: Fish-like conodonts, early ancestors of the vertebrates, appear.

Archaeon

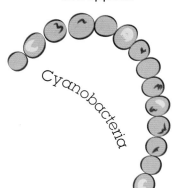

Cyanobacteria

Eoconodontus

Rhynia

Humans evolved very late in Earth's history, only around 350,000 years ago. Our species started to evolve from great apes, part of the primate order of mammals, between 4 and 7 million years ago. Today, we dominate the Earth, just as the dinosaurs once did. In the short time humans have been on Earth, we have changed the landscape by planting fields of crops and building factories and great cities.

Homo sapiens

470 million years ago: Plants are growing on land.

Ceratosaurus

Ichthyostega

367 million years ago: Four-legged animals, called tetrapods, evolve. Among the earliest are amphibians.

233 million years ago: A group of reptiles evolves into dinosaurs. By around 100 million years later, some dinosaurs have evolved into birds.

350,000 years ago: Humans are walking the Earth.

| 0.3 | 0.2 | 0.1 | 0.05 | 0.001 |

312 million years ago: Reptiles evolve from amphibians.

225 million years ago: Mammals evolve from reptiles.

55 million years ago: Large-brained mammals called primates evolve.

Darwinius

Scutosaurus

Megacerops

THEROPODS

The largest meat-eaters that ever walked the Earth were theropods. The theropods were a group of dinosaurs that evolved in the late Triassic Period, around 231 million years ago. Most theropods walked on their strong back legs, using their shorter front limbs for grabbing or slashing.

Nearly all meat-eating dinosaurs were theropods, but not every theropod was a meat-eater. Early theropods all ate meat, but over millions of years some evolved to eat plants, fish, or insects.

Theropods ranged in size from *Anchiornis*, just 34 cm (1 ft) long, to *Spinosaurus*, which reached 18 m (59 ft) long. There were several subgroups. Many of the largest theropods, including *Giganotosaurus* and *Carcharodontosaurus*, were in the carnosaur subgroup.

Another subgroup was the coelurosaurs, which included the ostrich-like *Ornithomimus* and the fierce *Tyrannosaurus*. Smaller coelurosaurs were covered in feathers. Other theropods probably had feathers only on some parts of their body, with most of their skin covered by small, bony scales.

Although most theropods were wiped out 66 million years ago, some coelurosaurs are alive today. Birds are descendants of small coelurosaurs that evolved to have wings.

Giganotosaurus lived around 98 million years ago. It grew up to 13 m (43 ft) long.

Theropod Skeletons

Theropods were saurischian (lizard-hipped) dinosaurs. They had hollow bones, like today's birds. The theropods take their name from the ancient Greek for "beast-footed," but their feet were more like those of birds than a lion's or bear's. Most theropods had three main toes, as well as three main fingers.

Like most theropods, *Ornithomimus* had three toes and fingers. However, this late theropod had no teeth. Its sharp beak was used for snapping up plants and small animals.

Carcharodontosaurus (left) and *Spinosaurus* were North African theropods, both of them too huge and ferocious to be attacked by smaller creatures.

A young *Coelophysis* snatches a fish from a stream, grasping the prey tightly in its long jaws.

COELOPHYSIDS

Coelophysids were fast runners, with light bones and small, slender bodies. Their front limbs were used for grasping prey. Coelophysids were early theropods, evolving in the late Triassic Period. The family is named after the dinosaur *Coelophysis*, which was first discovered in 1881 in the desert of the southwestern United States.

Coelophysids had large eyes, which faced forward, like the eyes of modern birds of prey such as eagles and hawks. Like those birds, coelophysids could probably spot fast-moving prey at a distance.

These dinosaurs had very sharp, backward-curving teeth, with jagged edges to help with slicing through flesh. Most coelophysids preyed on lizards and other land animals much smaller than themselves. However, fossils show us that *Coelophysis*'s teeth had horizontal ridges when it was young, which would have helped with catching slippery fish. Its teeth changed shape as it grew older, suggesting *Coelophysis* also changed its diet.

The bones of large groups of coelophysids have been found together, making some paleontologists think these dinosaurs lived and hunted in packs. However, other paleontologists think the dinosaurs might just have been caught by the same sudden flood or other disaster, resulting in their bodies being buried together.

Camposaurus lived around 220 million years ago in what is today the United States.

Family:	Coelophysidae
Range:	North America, South America, Europe, Asia, and Africa
Time Period:	Late Triassic to early Jurassic, 220–183 million years ago
Size Range:	1–3 m (3.3–9.8 ft) long

Procompsognathus

Coelophysis

COMPSOGNATHIDS

These theropods are among the smallest dinosaurs ever discovered. Compsognathids were fast-moving hunters of little animals such as lizards and insects. Fossils of compsognathid stomachs show that they sometimes swallowed their prey whole. The long tails of these dinosaurs were used for balance during quick turns and leaps.

Fossils show that some members of the Compsognathidae family had feathers, alongside scales on their back legs or tails. Feathers and scales are made from the same material, keratin, which is also in human hair and nails.

Compsognathids were probably some of the earliest dinosaurs to grow feathers. Before this development, all dinosaurs just had scales. Dinosaurs probably started to grow feathers because they helped keep them warm. These early feathers were simpler than the long, branching feathers of today's birds.

This family takes its name from the dinosaur *Compsognathus*, which was discovered in 1859. *Compsognathus* was named after the ancient Greek words for "elegant jaw" because of its long, pointed snout. So far, no fossils have been found showing that *Compsognathus* had feathers like some of its relatives. This may be because feathers are fossilized only in particular types of rocks, so we are not left with evidence of most feathering.

Sinosauropteryx had simple feathers over most of its body, as well as areas of scales. In 1996, a Sinosauropteryx fossil was one of the first dinosaur fossils found showing feathers.

Family:	Compsognathidae
Range:	South America, Europe, and Asia
Time Period:	Late Jurassic to early Cretaceous, 151.5–108 million years ago
Size Range:	0.75–1.8 m (2.5–5.9 ft) long

Juravenator

Huaxiagnathus

Compsognathus lived on sunny islands in the ancient Tethys Sea, where it may have been one of the largest predators, despite its small size.

SPINOSAURS

These huge predators had crocodile-like jaws lined with sharp teeth. Like crocodiles, some spinosaurs could both walk on land and swim in rivers, lakes, and shallow seas. They snapped up prey ranging from fish to other dinosaurs and flying reptiles. Unlike most theropods, spinosaurs had large, strong front limbs, so they may have walked on four legs.

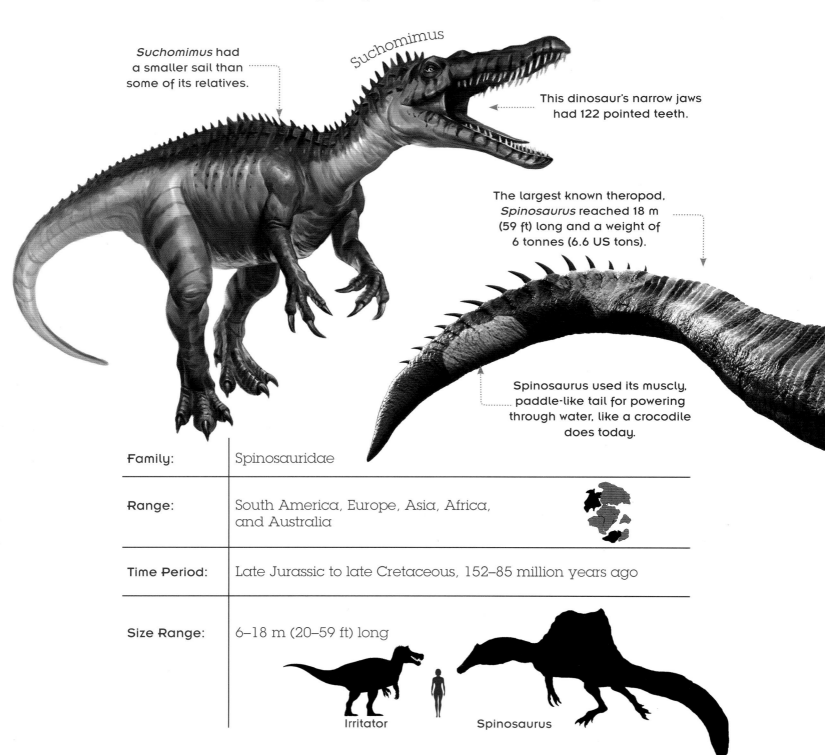

Suchomimus had a smaller sail than some of its relatives.

Suchomimus

This dinosaur's narrow jaws had 122 pointed teeth.

The largest known theropod, *Spinosaurus* reached 18 m (59 ft) long and a weight of 6 tonnes (6.6 US tons).

Spinosaurus used its muscly, paddle-like tail for powering through water, like a crocodile does today.

Family:	Spinosauridae
Range:	South America, Europe, Asia, Africa, and Australia
Time Period:	Late Jurassic to late Cretaceous, 152–85 million years ago
Size Range:	6–18 m (20–59 ft) long

Irritator   Spinosaurus

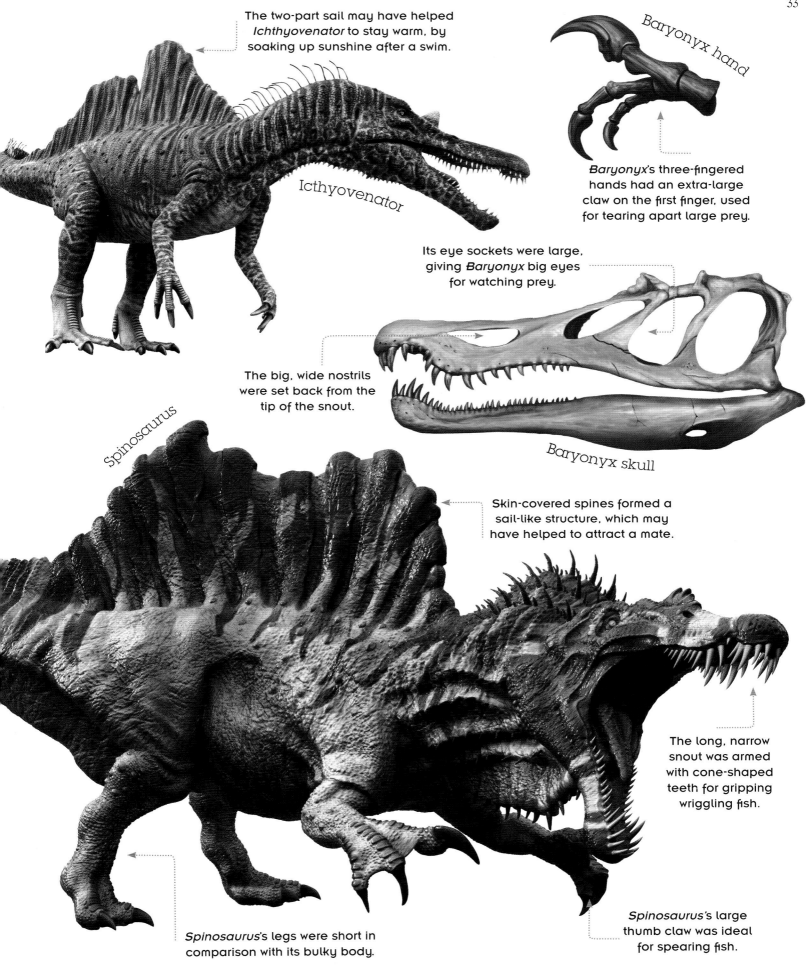

The two-part sail may have helped *Ichthyovenator* to stay warm, by soaking up sunshine after a swim.

Icthyovenator

Baryonyx hand

Baryonyx's three-fingered hands had an extra-large claw on the first finger, used for tearing apart large prey.

Its eye sockets were large, giving *Baryonyx* big eyes for watching prey.

The big, wide nostrils were set back from the tip of the snout.

Baryonyx skull

Spinosaurus

Skin-covered spines formed a sail-like structure, which may have helped to attract a mate.

The long, narrow snout was armed with cone-shaped teeth for gripping wriggling fish.

Spinosaurus's legs were short in comparison with its bulky body.

Spinosaurus's large thumb claw was ideal for spearing fish.

DINOSAUR DIETS

The earliest dinosaurs were meat-eaters (carnivores). Over millions of years, some dinosaurs became plant-eaters (herbivores) or ate whatever they found (omnivores). Around two-thirds of all dinosaurs were plant-eaters. Today, there are also fewer meat-eating animals than plant-eaters, as well as fewer plant-eaters than plants, so there is enough food to go around.

Paleontologists have compared dinosaur teeth and jaws with those of modern animals, such as meat-eating lions and plant-eating deer. They believe that animals with similar-shaped teeth have similar diets. Like lions, carnivorous dinosaurs had large, strong jaws and sharp teeth. Like modern plant-eaters, herbivorous dinosaurs had teeth suited to the particular plants they ate, whether they were soft-leaved or tough-stemmed. Some dinosaurs had no teeth, so they probably used their hard, beak-like jaws to crop plants or seize small animals.

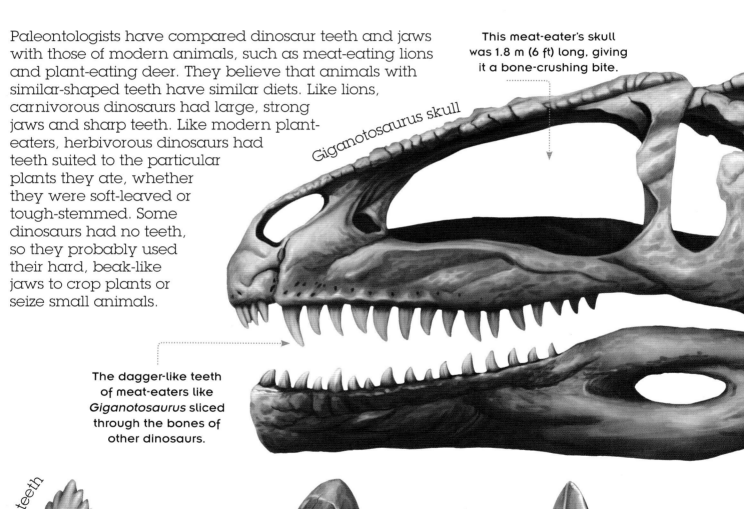

Giganotosaurus skull

This meat-eater's skull was 1.8 m (6 ft) long, giving it a bone-crushing bite.

The dagger-like teeth of meat-eaters like *Giganotosaurus* sliced through the bones of other dinosaurs.

Plant-eaters' teeth

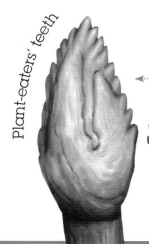

The sauropod *Rebbachisaurus* had leaf-shaped teeth for chewing soft plants such as ferns.

The sauropod *Camarasaurus* had spoon-shaped teeth for stripping leaves from stems.

Iguanodon teeth could grind tough tree leaves and twigs.

A few fossilized dinosaur stomachs have been found. These can tell us exactly what a dinosaur ate, as well as whether it chewed its food or swallowed it whole. Fossilized poops, called coprolites, contain fragments of what dinosaurs ate. It is not easy to match a coprolite to the dinosaur that created it, but coprolite size, shape, and location can give clues.

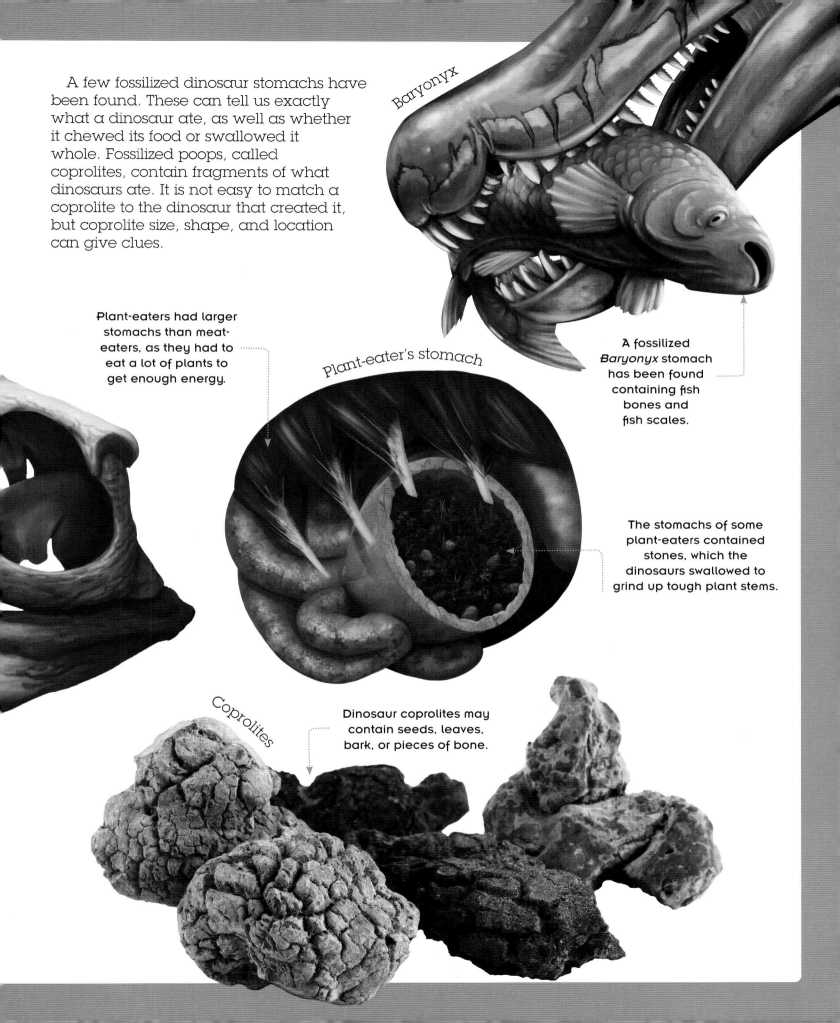

Baryonyx

A fossilized *Baryonyx* stomach has been found containing fish bones and fish scales.

Plant-eaters had larger stomachs than meat-eaters, as they had to eat a lot of plants to get enough energy.

Plant-eater's stomach

The stomachs of some plant-eaters contained stones, which the dinosaurs swallowed to grind up tough plant stems.

Coprolites

Dinosaur coprolites may contain seeds, leaves, bark, or pieces of bone.

A *Diplodocus* is attacked by a hungry *Allosaurus* pack in Jurassic North America.

ALLOSAURS

With their jagged-edged teeth, allosaurs sliced chunks of flesh out of their prey, often snapping so viciously that they left broken teeth by the bodies of their victims. Until the evolution of the tyrannosaurs around 75 million years later, the allosaurs were the largest and deadliest predators in North America. They were members of the carnosaur subgroup.

The bodies of several allosaurs have often been found side by side, which suggests these dinosaurs hunted together, particularly if they were bringing down large prey, such as a *Diplodocus*. However, some allosaur fossils have bites on their skulls from other members of their species. This makes some paleontologists think allosaurs were too aggressive to work together.

Allosaurs had a horn above each eye, as well as ridges running along the sides of their nose. Like today's animals with horns or antlers, such as deer, these features may have been used to attract a mate.

Despite their big skulls, allosaurs may have had weaker jaw muscles and weaker bites than today's crocodiles and lions. Allosaurs probably fed by jabbing their narrow jaws into prey, then ripping out flesh by pulling with their clamped teeth. As well as hunting live prey, allosaurs probably fed on dead animals they came across.

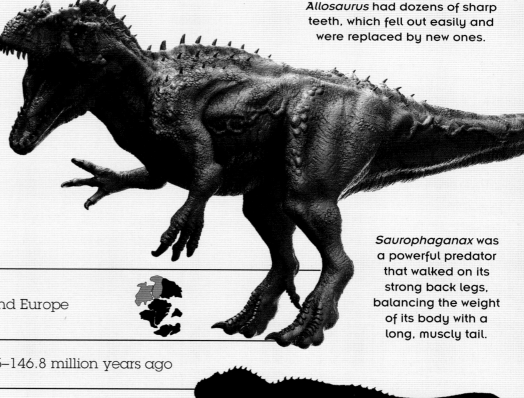

Allosaurus had dozens of sharp teeth, which fell out easily and were replaced by new ones.

Saurophaganax was a powerful predator that walked on its strong back legs, balancing the weight of its body with a long, muscly tail.

Family:	Allosauridae
Range:	North America and Europe
Time Period:	Late Jurassic, 155–146.8 million years ago
Size Range:	8–13 m (26–43 ft) long

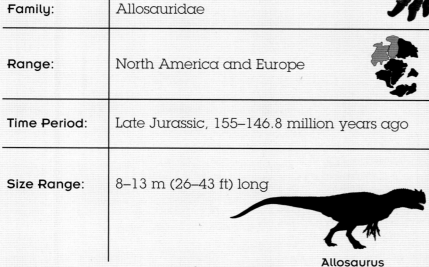

Allosaurus   Saurophaganax

DROMAEOSAURS

Dromaeosaurs were covered in feathers, with soft, short feathers on their body and longer ones on their arms and tails. These dinosaurs had longer arms than most theropods. Some dromaeosaurs could fold their arms against their body, like wings. A few dromaeosaurs might even have used these wings for gliding down from branches or for short flapping flights.

Around 70 curved, knife-like teeth were used to attack smaller dinosaurs.

Deinonychus

Deinonychus probably could not fly, but may have flapped its wings for balance when jumping on prey.

Protoceratops is defending itself by biting *Velociraptor*'s arm.

Deinonychus held its second toe off the ground to protect its large claw, used for pinning down prey.

Long, strong legs made this dinosaur a good runner, but not as fast as modern flightless birds such as ostriches.

Velociraptor

In 1971, a fossil was found of a *Velociraptor* attacking a *Protoceratops*, just as they were both buried by a landslide.

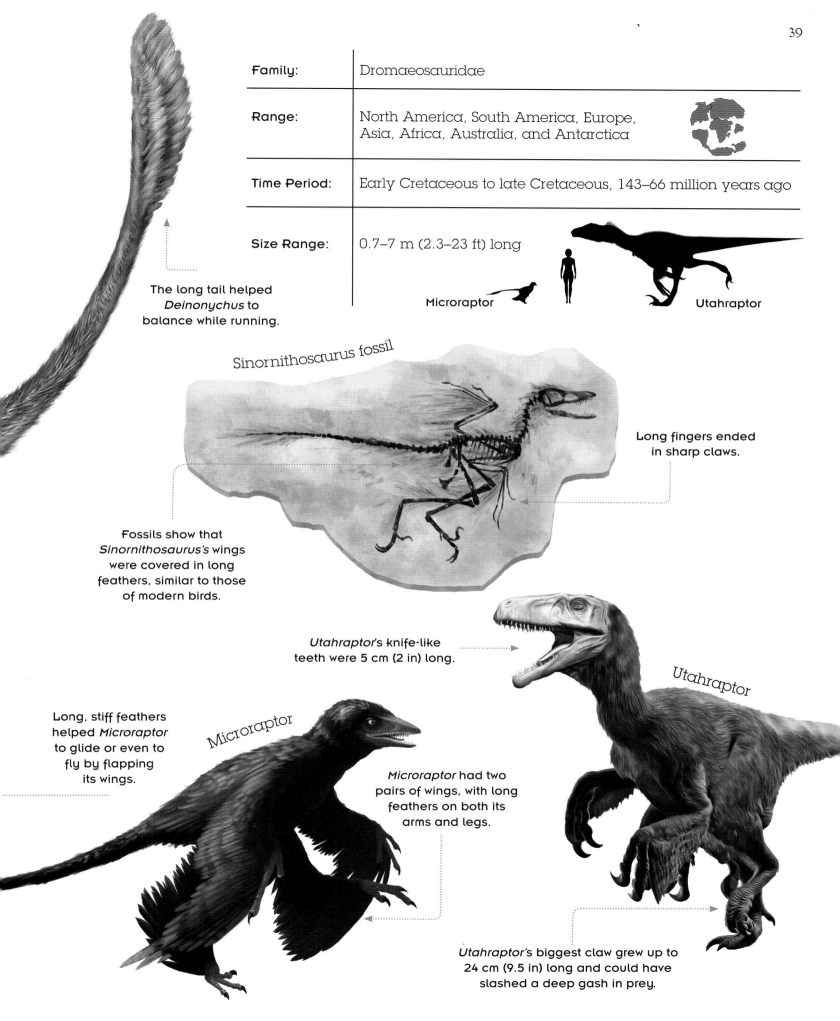

Family:	Dromaeosauridae
Range:	North America, South America, Europe, Asia, Africa, Australia, and Antarctica
Time Period:	Early Cretaceous to late Cretaceous, 143–66 million years ago
Size Range:	0.7–7 m (2.3–23 ft) long

Microraptor

Utahraptor

The long tail helped *Deinonychus* to balance while running.

Sinornithosaurus fossil

Long fingers ended in sharp claws.

Fossils show that *Sinornithosaurus's* wings were covered in long feathers, similar to those of modern birds.

Utahraptor's knife-like teeth were 5 cm (2 in) long.

Utahraptor

Long, stiff feathers helped *Microraptor* to glide or even to fly by flapping its wings.

Microraptor

Microraptor had two pairs of wings, with long feathers on both its arms and legs.

Utahraptor's biggest claw grew up to 24 cm (9.5 in) long and could have slashed a deep gash in prey.

Living 68–66 million years ago, *Tyrannosaurus rex* weighed up to 14 tonnes (15.4 US tons), a little more than *Triceratops* (left) and twice as much as today's elephants.

TYRANNOSAURS

Tyrannosaurs had massive skulls with up to 70 long, spiky teeth. They walked upright on their strong hind legs. Most tyrannosaurs were the largest meat-eaters in their region, so only sick, young, or old individuals would have faced attack. The largest tyrannosaur of all was *Tyrannosaurus rex*, one of the biggest meat-eaters that has ever walked the Earth.

Many scientists think tyrannosaurs were both hunters and scavengers. Scavengers eat animals they find dead or dying. Some of today's big meat-eaters, such as lions, are also both hunters and scavengers. *Tyrannosaurus rex* needed to feed often, so it probably ate whatever animals it came across, alive or dead.

Tyrannosaurs may have run at 15 to 30 km (9 to 18 miles) per hour. This was much slower than smaller, lighter theropods such as dromaeosaurs, but fast enough to catch slow-moving plant-eaters such as ceratopsians.

A tyrannosaur's front limbs were very short compared with its body size. However, these arms had two viciously sharp claws. Tyrannosaurs probably slashed with their arms while grasping prey in their jaws.

Bite marks in fossils are evidence that tyrannosaurs sometimes fought each other. Young tyrannosaurs may have honed their skills by play fighting. Older dinosaurs may have fought each other to the death.

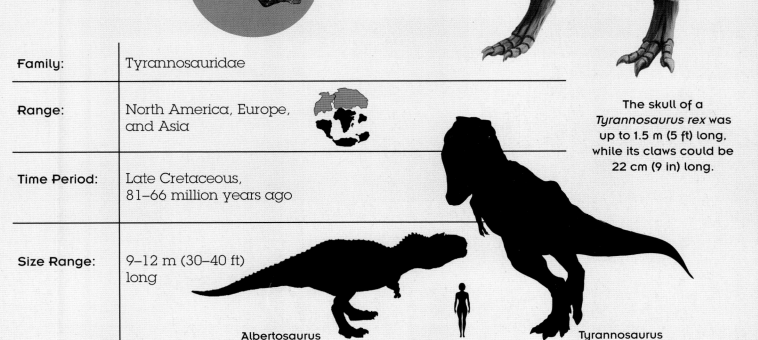

Family:	Tyrannosauridae
Range:	North America, Europe, and Asia
Time Period:	Late Cretaceous, 81–66 million years ago
Size Range:	9–12 m (30–40 ft) long

The skull of a *Tyrannosaurus rex* was up to 1.5 m (5 ft) long, while its claws could be 22 cm (9 in) long.

Albertosaurus

Tyrannosaurus

THERIZINOSAURS

These dinosaurs are named after the ancient Greek words for "cutting" (*therizo*) and "lizard" (*sauros*) because of the giant curved claws on their hands. *Therizinosaurus* had the longest known claws of any animal that has ever lived, reaching up to 1 m (3.3 ft) in length. However, these claws were not used for hunting other animals, as therizinosaurs were probably plant-eaters.

Therizinosaurs had much longer and more flexible arms than other theropods. Paleontologists believe these dinosaurs used their arms and long claws for hooking and pulling down high tree branches so they could feed on leaves. Their long necks also helped them feed up high. This meant that therizinosaurs did not compete with most other local plant-eaters for food.

Although therizinosaurs did not use their claws for attacking, large claws would have been useful to defend themselves against fiercer theropods. It is possible that therizinosaurs also used their claws for attracting a mate, with bigger claws being more popular.

Unlike most dinosaurs, therizinosaurs had ears rather like those of modern birds, enabling them to hear higher sounds and to be good at working out which direction sounds were coming from. This may have been useful in hearing the cries of young therizinosaurs and the approach of predators.

Beipiaosaurus was an early therizinosaur. Its body was covered in soft, short feathers, while longer feathers grew from its arms and tail.

Family:	Therizinosauridae
Range:	North America, Europe, Asia, and Africa
Time Period:	Late Cretaceous, 94–66 million years ago
Size Range:	2.3–10 m (7.5–33 ft) long

Neimongosaurus

Therizinosaurus

Therizinosaurus had a strong beak-like mouth for cropping leaves, as well as leaf-shaped teeth for chewing.

EVOLUTION OF BIRDS

Today, there are around 10,000 species of birds, from plant-eating pigeons to meat-eating eagles. All these birds are the descendants of theropod dinosaurs. Over millions of years, some dinosaurs evolved to have more and more birdlike features: smaller bodies, feathers, toothless beaks, and long arms that could be flapped as wings.

Around 160 million years ago, some small, long-armed, feathered coelurosaur theropods started to climb into trees to hide from predators or look for leaves and insects that were not reachable from the ground. After a while, some of these bird-like dinosaurs were able to glide down from trees, by opening wide their long, feathered arms. Eventually, bird-like dinosaurs could flap their wings to fly longer distances. By 130 million years ago, the first true birds were soaring through the sky.

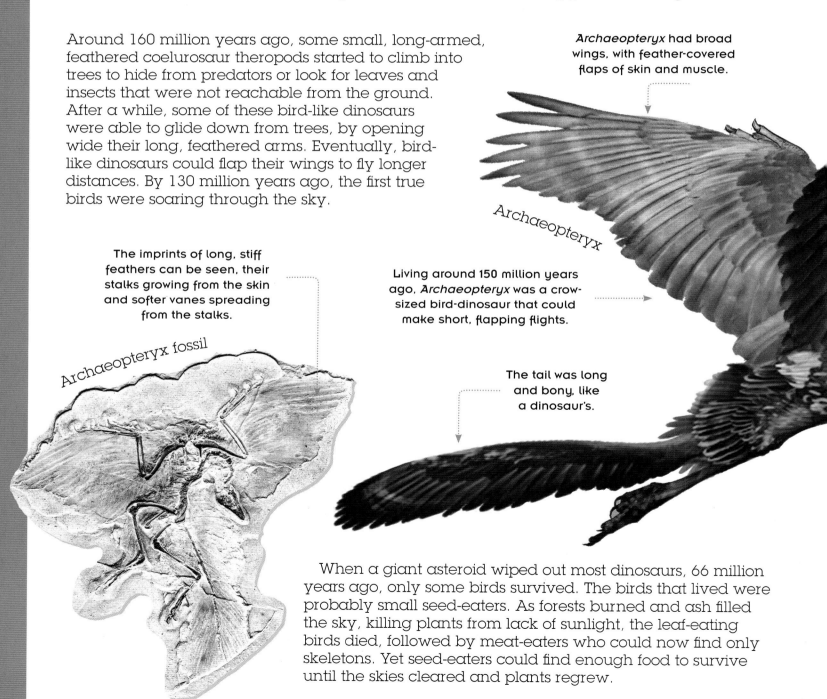

Archaeopteryx had broad wings, with feather-covered flaps of skin and muscle.

Archaeopteryx

The imprints of long, stiff feathers can be seen, their stalks growing from the skin and softer vanes spreading from the stalks.

Archaeopteryx fossil

Living around 150 million years ago, *Archaeopteryx* was a crow-sized bird-dinosaur that could make short, flapping flights.

The tail was long and bony, like a dinosaur's.

When a giant asteroid wiped out most dinosaurs, 66 million years ago, only some birds survived. The birds that lived were probably small seed-eaters. As forests burned and ash filled the sky, killing plants from lack of sunlight, the leaf-eating birds died, followed by meat-eaters who could now find only skeletons. Yet seed-eaters could find enough food to survive until the skies cleared and plants regrew.

Around 160 million years ago, *Anchiornis* was a bird-like theropod dinosaur that probably could not fly.

Anchiornis

Paleontologists disagree on whether *Caudipteryx* was a flightless bird, like a modern ostrich, or a theropod dinosaur.

The fingers ended in claws, a feature lost by modern birds.

Caudipteryx

Like most dinosaurs but unlike modern birds, *Archaeopteryx* had teeth.

Caudipteryx lived around 125 million years ago.

Living around 125 million years ago, *Iberomesornis* still had a single claw on each wing, but it had a shorter, more bird-like tail.

This bird was named *Iberomesornis* ("Spanish middle bird") because its body shape was halfway between *Archaeopteryx* and modern birds.

Iberomesornis

SAUROPODOMORPHS

The sauropodomorphs were plant-eaters with long necks and tails. Early sauropodomorphs were small and slender. Over millions of years, these dinosaurs became larger and heavier. Eventually, sauropodomorphs were larger than any other land animal that has ever lived.

When sauropodomorphs first evolved, around 231 million years ago, they were light enough to walk just on their two back legs. These early sauropodomorphs may have been omnivores, eating both plants and small animals. Millions of years before, their ancestors had only eaten meat. In fact, sauropodomorphs shared the same meat-eating ancestors as fierce theropods such as tyrannosaurs. Like theropods, sauropodomorphs were saurischian ("lizard-hipped") dinosaurs.

Over time, as the sauropodomorphs adapted to eating only plants, they grew bigger and developed longer and longer necks. Their necks enabled them to reach high or distant plants, so they did not need to compete with smaller plant-eaters. Their huge body size protected them from all but the largest meat-eaters.

Like modern large animals, such as elephants, the sauropodomorphs were now far too heavy to balance only on their back legs. They walked slowly on their four sturdy legs, their long tails balancing their long necks.

Living around 214–204 million years ago, *Plateosaurus* was a small, early sauropodomorph that walked on its back legs.

Sauropodomorph Necks

Sauropodomorph necks reached over 15 m (49 ft) long. For these dinosaurs to lift such long necks, the neck and skull bones needed to be extremely light. Sauropodomorph skulls were very small compared to their bodies. The bones of the neck, called vertebrae, had many large air-filled spaces.

Apatosaurus had 15 air-filled vertebrae in its neck. Modern giraffes, as well as humans, have just seven vertebrae.

Up to 34 m (112 ft) long and 18 m (59 ft) high, *Sauroposeidon* was the tallest known dinosaur. It lived on the shores of the Gulf of Mexico around 112 million years ago.

In Triassic South Africa, a frightened *Melanorosaurus* is helpless when cornered by a sharp-toothed, crocodile-like rauisuchian reptile.

MELANOROSAURS

First evolving around 227 million years ago, these sauropodomorphs were among the earliest of the huge plant-eaters. Although not as immense as later sauropodomorphs, they were still some of the biggest land animals of their day. Melanorosaurs had bulky bodies, with four thick, muscular legs to take their weight.

The melanorosaurs had much shorter necks than their later relatives. They probably fed on low-growing plants, but might have reared up on their back legs to reach higher branches. Although melanorosaurs walked on all fours, their front legs ended in awkward hand-like feet, a reminder that their ancestors had walked only on their back legs.

Melanorosaurs were largely plant-eaters, but they may have snapped up insects and other small animals from time to time. At the front of a melanorosaur's top jaw were a few sharp, pointed teeth, which could have bitten struggling creatures. The rest of its mouth held many leaf-shaped teeth with jagged edges, which were perfect for ripping plants. Later sauropodomorphs, which only ever ate plants, no longer had those pointed front teeth.

The melanorosaur family is named after the species *Melanorosaurus* (from the ancient Greek for "black mountain lizard"). This dinosaur was named in 1924 after the Thaba 'Nyama (Black Mountain) in South Africa, where its fossils were found.

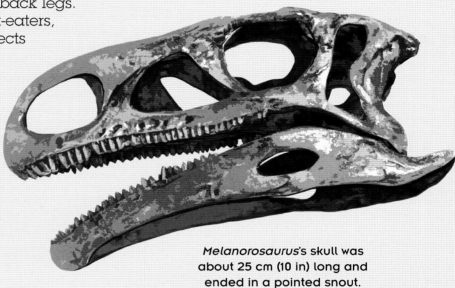

Melanorosaurus's skull was about 25 cm (10 in) long and ended in a pointed snout.

Family:	Melanorosauridae
Range:	Europe and Africa
Time Period:	Late Triassic to early Jurassic, 227–189 million years ago
Size Range:	8–11 m (26–36 ft) long

Melanorosaurus   Camelotia

DIPLODOCIDS

Diplodocids were extremely long, but had a slimmer build than other enormous sauropodomorphs. These plant-eaters had teeth only at the front of their mouth. The peg-like teeth were used to pluck leaves, which were gulped down without chewing. Diplodocids also swallowed stones to grind leaves inside their stomach.

Supersaurus

Diplodocus

Supersaurus probably could not lift its 12-m (39-ft) neck very high, instead using it to reach for leaves over a wide area.

Its front legs were shorter than its back legs, giving its shoulders a downward slope.

Supersaurus stood 5.5 m (18 ft) tall at the shoulder.

Diplodocus lived 154–152 million years ago in North America.

The first toe on each foot had a long claw that could be used against attackers.

From snout to tail tip, *Diplodocus* was around 32 m (105 ft) long.

This dinosaur's four strong legs supported its weight of up to 16 tonnes (17.6 US tons), more than three times the weight of an African bush elephant.

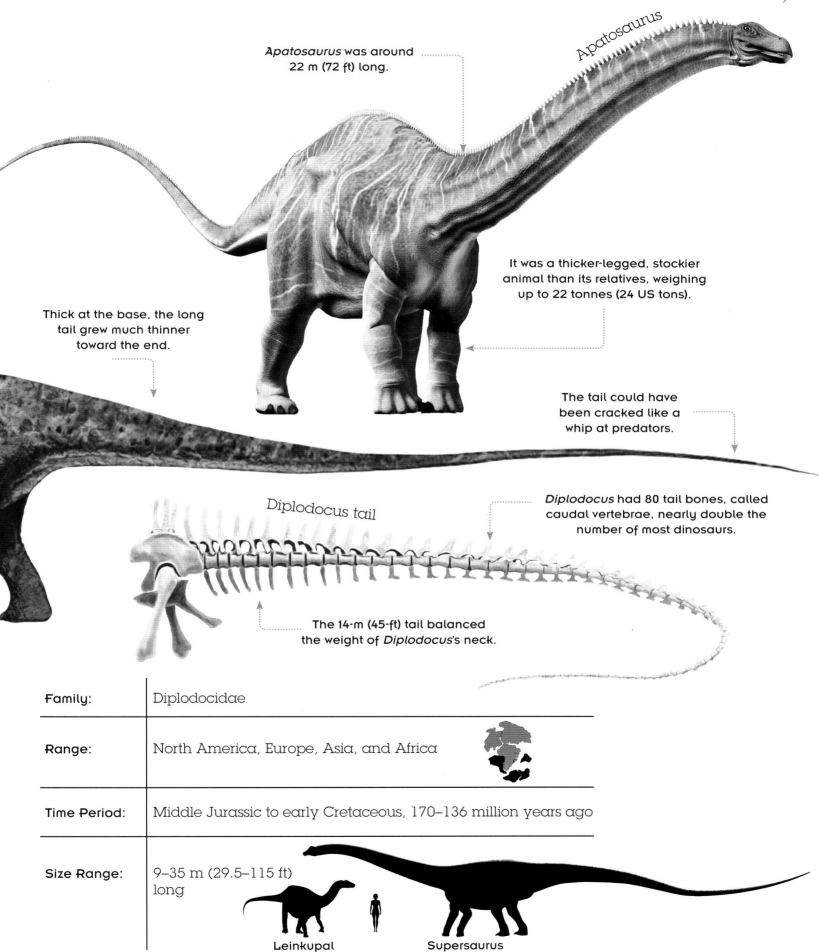

Apatosaurus

Apatosaurus was around 22 m (72 ft) long.

It was a thicker-legged, stockier animal than its relatives, weighing up to 22 tonnes (24 US tons).

Thick at the base, the long tail grew much thinner toward the end.

The tail could have been cracked like a whip at predators.

Diplodocus tail

Diplodocus had 80 tail bones, called caudal vertebrae, nearly double the number of most dinosaurs.

The 14-m (45-ft) tail balanced the weight of *Diplodocus*'s neck.

Family:	Diplodocidae
Range:	North America, Europe, Asia, and Africa
Time Period:	Middle Jurassic to early Cretaceous, 170–136 million years ago
Size Range:	9–35 m (29.5–115 ft) long

Leinkupal

Supersaurus

DINOSAUR HERDS

Many plant-eating dinosaurs lived in herds, which offered them some safety from predators. In a herd, many eyes and ears are on the alert for danger. During an attack, the herd can claw and bite together—or can scatter in all directions, confusing the predator. Some meat-eaters may also have lived together, hunting in packs to bring down large prey.

There is plenty of fossil evidence that some dinosaurs lived in herds, particularly plant-eaters such as sauropodomorphs and cerapods. Footprints show large numbers of dinosaurs walking together, with smaller, younger dinosaurs walking in the middle of the herd for safety. The bones of groups of dinosaurs, often of different ages, have also been found together. Some groups contained only young dinosaurs, which may have stayed together till they were fully grown. In China, the bodies of 20 young *Sinornithomimus* theropods were found together, after they got stuck in mud. All the dinosaurs were between one and seven years old.

The meat-eater *Shaochilong* lived in China in the late Cretaceous period.

Young Sinornithomimus herd

Diplodocus herd

Diplodocus herds roamed North America in the late Jurassic Period.

A young *Diplodocus* stays in the middle of the herd.

In some cases, paleontologists cannot know for sure if the dinosaurs were a herd or whether they just happened to be together at a feeding or drinking spot when a sudden disaster, such as a landslide, struck. When the bodies of meat-eaters are found around the body of their prey, it may not be the case that the animals were working together. The meat-eaters may actually have been fighting over the body. However, the high number of fossilized groups suggests that many dinosaurs did come together to nest, feed, sleep, or travel between grazing areas.

Out of sight of their parents, a group of young *Sinornithomimus* scatters and runs.

DICRAEOSAURS

These dinosaurs had smaller bodies and shorter necks than most Jurassic and Cretaceous sauropodomorphs. Dicraeosaurs had long spikes sticking up from the bones of their necks and backs. In some species, these spines were covered in skin and muscle, while in others they formed a comb-like crest.

The longest neck and back spines of any dicraeosaur belonged to *Amargasaurus*, which lived in South America around 129–122 million years ago. It had a double row of spines, up to 60 cm (24 in) long. Paleontologists are not sure whether the spines were covered by skin.

If *Amargasaurus*'s spines were covered, they might have protected an air bag, which was connected to the lungs to help with breathing. If the spines were not covered, they might have been used to pierce predators by suddenly bending the neck downward during an attack. The modern Arabian oryx uses its horns in this way to defend itself against lions.

With their short necks, the dicraeosaurs probably fed on plants no more than 3 m (9.8 ft) off the ground. The shortest neck in the family, around 2 m (6.6 ft) long, belonged to the South American

Brachytrachelopan. While most Jurassic and Cretaceous sauropodomorphs specialized in eating high plants, the dicraeosaur family avoided competition by eating at mid-height.

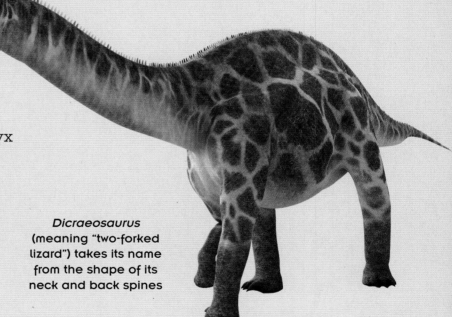

Dicraeosaurus (meaning "two-forked lizard") takes its name from the shape of its neck and back spines

Family:	Dicraeosauridae
Range:	North America, South America, Asia, and Africa
Time Period:	Middle Jurassic to early Cretaceous, 174–122 million years ago
Size Range:	10–12 m (33–39 ft) long

Brachytrachelopan   Dicraeosaurus

With a neck around 2.4 m (7.9 ft) long, an adult *Amargasaurus* fed on mid-level plants such as gingkos and cycads.

In a Cretaceous Chinese swamp, a *Mamenchisaurus* herd feeds on ferns, while *Boreopterus* pterosaurs search for small prey.

MAMENCHISAURS

Manenchisaurs had exceptionally lengthy necks, up to 15 m (49 ft) long, making up nearly half their total body length. The species *Mamenchisaurus* had 19 vertebrae in its neck, 9 more than a *Tyrannosaurus*. Their necks meant that mamenchisaurs did not have to move their weighty body as they reached for food, saving precious energy.

The shape of mamenchisaur neck bones and muscles probably meant they could not lift their heads high to feed in trees. Instead, mamenchisaurs probably reached to distant clumps of low plants, an ability that would have been particularly useful for avoiding swampy ground. Mamenchisaur skulls were small, so they could be supported by their slender necks. Yet since these dinosaurs had to eat large amounts of plant material to survive, their jaws were as big as possible. The jaw joint, or hinge, was nearly at the back of the skull. Mamenchisaur jaws were armed with wide, blunt teeth, which could have gathered big bundles of leaves in one grab.

When these dinosaurs hatched from their eggs, they probably weighed as much as a human baby, around 4 kg (8.8 lb). By constant eating while awake, a *Mamenchisaurus* could have gained more than 2,000 kg (4,400 lb) per year, reaching its full weight, around 70,000 kg (155,000 lb), by the age of 30.

Omeisaurus ate up to 1,000 kg (2,200 lb) of ferns and other plants every day. By the time it was around 30 years old, it was 20 m (65.6 ft) long.

Family:	Mamenchisauridae
Range:	Asia and Africa
Time Period:	Early Jurassic to early Cretaceous, 184–114 million years ago
Size Range:	12–35 m (39–115 ft) long

Tonganosaurus

Mamenchisaurus

DINOSAUR EGGS

Dinosaurs laid eggs with hard shells, like modern birds. Females usually laid between 10 and 30 eggs in a nest, which was sometimes shared with other members of a herd. Nests were made by scraping a hollow in the ground, digging a burrow, or building a mound to bury the eggs for warmth.

While most dinosaurs laid quite round eggs, the meat-eating theropods laid long eggs with rounded ends. The smallest dinosaurs, such as the chicken-sized *Sinosauropteryx*, laid eggs smaller than a chicken egg. The largest dinosaur eggs ever found were 60 cm (24 in) long and probably belonged to a large theropod like *Gigantoraptor*, which was about 8 m (26 ft) long as an adult. Many of the biggest dinosaurs were tiny when they hatched: the 5-m (16-ft) sauropodomorph *Massospondylus* started life just 15 cm (6 in) long.

These round eggs belonged to a plant-eating dinosaur.

Eggs were often laid in a circle.

Fossilized dinosaur eggs

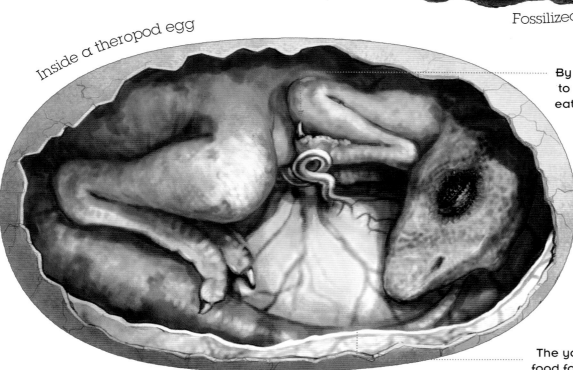

Inside a theropod egg

By the time it was ready to hatch, a baby meat-eating dinosaur already had claws.

The yolk sac is filled with food for the growing baby.

Many dinosaurs watched over their nests, with either mothers or fathers perhaps sitting on the eggs to keep them warm until they hatched. Some dinosaurs, such as the plant-eating cerapod *Maiasura*, took care of their babies after they were born. Such babies may have been toothless and needed help to feed themselves. Other dinosaurs, including some theropods, may have buried their eggs then walked away. When these eggs hatched, the babies probably already had teeth and claws and were able to fend for themselves.

Citipati's feathered arms were spread over the eggs to keep them warm, when it was probably buried by a sandstorm.

A fossil was found showing the theropod *Citipati* sitting on its nest.

Citipati nest

Fossils have been discovered of a *Maiasaura* nesting colony, where the herd laid their eggs and took care of their young.

Maiasaura family

Fossilized footprints tell us that *Maiasaura* babies stayed close to their parents until they were around a year old.

BRACHIOSAURS

These dinosaurs had much longer front legs than back legs, resulting in the name brachiosaurs, which means "arm lizards" in ancient Greek. When at rest, their necks were held diagonally, at an angle of 45 degrees, to the ground. With heights of up to 12 m (39 ft), brachiosaurs could have reached higher branches than many sauropodomorphs.

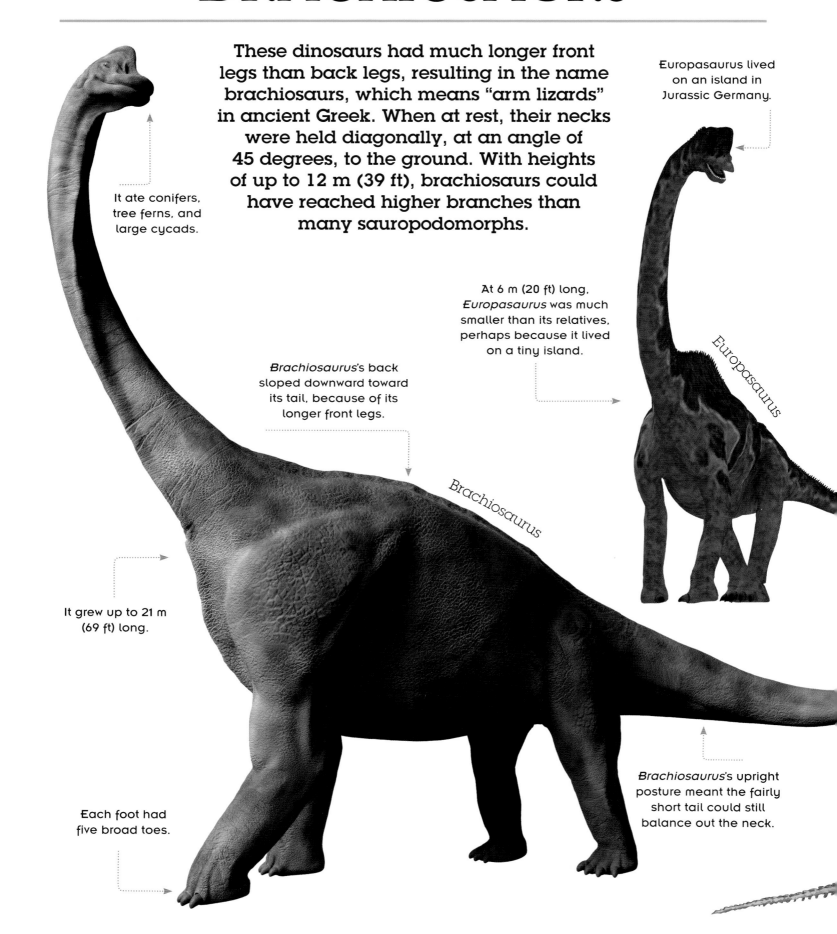

It ate conifers, tree ferns, and large cycads.

Europasaurus lived on an island in Jurassic Germany.

At 6 m (20 ft) long, *Europasaurus* was much smaller than its relatives, perhaps because it lived on a tiny island.

Brachiosaurus's back sloped downward toward its tail, because of its longer front legs.

Europasaurus

Brachiosaurus

It grew up to 21 m (69 ft) long.

Brachiosaurus's upright posture meant the fairly short tail could still balance out the neck.

Each foot had five broad toes.

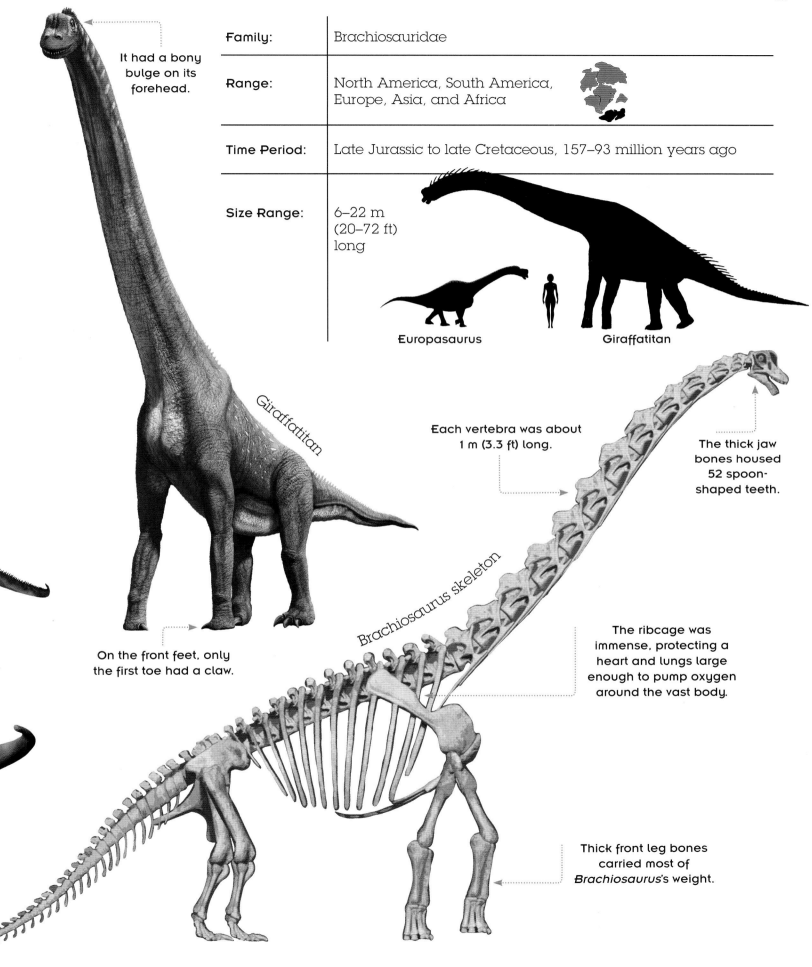

It had a bony bulge on its forehead.

Family:	Brachiosauridae
Range:	North America, South America, Europe, Asia, and Africa
Time Period:	Late Jurassic to late Cretaceous, 157–93 million years ago
Size Range:	6–22 m (20–72 ft) long

Europasaurus

Giraffatitan

Giraffatitan

Each vertebra was about 1 m (3.3 ft) long.

The thick jaw bones housed 52 spoon-shaped teeth.

Brachiosaurus skeleton

The ribcage was immense, protecting a heart and lungs large enough to pump oxygen around the vast body.

On the front feet, only the first toe had a claw.

Thick front leg bones carried most of Brachiosaurus's weight.

Even predators as large as *Giganotosaurus* might have needed to work as a pack to bring down a giant like *Argentinosaurus*.

COLOSSOSAURS

The colossosaurs included the enormous dinosaur that was possibly the largest land animal of all time: *Argentinosaurus*. It is believed to have grown up to 39.7 m (130 ft) long, about as long as nine family cars end to end. The colossosaurs (which means "giant lizards" in ancient Greek) lived in South America.

Argentinosaurus's size has been estimated by studying the few bones that have been found, including a thigh bone 2.5 m (8.2 ft) long. A close relative of *Argentinosaurus* was *Patagotitan*, the second longest known dinosaur, which is estimated to have reached 37 m (121 ft).

Colossosaurs' great size would have helped them fend off attacks from all but the largest meat-eating dinosaurs.

However, alongside these great South American plant-eaters, immense theropods evolved to prey on them, including *Mapusaurus* and *Giganotosaurus*, which were both over 10 m (33 ft) long.

Another advantage to being so huge was that there was plenty of room in a colossosaur's body for a gargantuan stomach and extremely long intestines. It would have taken up to two weeks for food to travel the length of the intestines. During all this time, the goodness from the food was being absorbed by the dinosaur's body, so it was able to gain every last bit of energy.

Patagotitan may have weighed up to 77 tonnes (85 US tons), more than a dozen African elephants.

Family:	Colossosauridae
Range:	South America
Time Period:	Late Cretaceous, 101–92 million years ago
Size Range:	11–39.7 m (36–130 ft) long

Rinconsaurus   Argentinosaurus

SALTASAURS

Although the saltasaurs were large beasts, they were usually smaller than other sauropodomorphs of their time. For extra protection, many had bony plates across their back. The largest dinosaur in the family, *Alamosaurus*, was the last sauropodomorph to become extinct, when a giant asteroid hit Earth 66 million years ago.

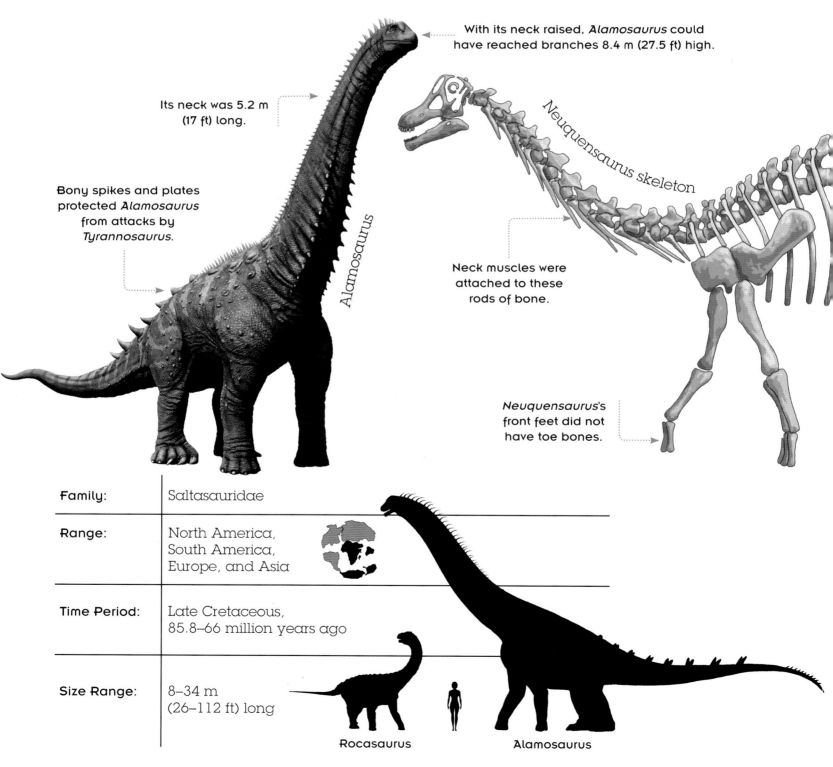

With its neck raised, *Alamosaurus* could have reached branches 8.4 m (27.5 ft) high.

Its neck was 5.2 m (17 ft) long.

Bony spikes and plates protected *Alamosaurus* from attacks by *Tyrannosaurus*.

Alamosaurus

Neuquensaurus skeleton

Neck muscles were attached to these rods of bone.

Neuquensaurus's front feet did not have toe bones.

Family:	Saltasauridae
Range:	North America, South America, Europe, and Asia
Time Period:	Late Cretaceous, 85.8–66 million years ago
Size Range:	8–34 m (26–112 ft) long

Rocasaurus

Alamosaurus

Peg-like teeth were useful for stripping leaves from branches but not for chewing.

Saltasaurus could rear up on its back legs to reach higher branches.

Saltasaurus feeding

Wide, strong hip bones allowed *Neuquensaurus* to balance on its back legs to feed.

Leaves stayed in *Saltasaurus*'s stomach for a long time, slowly being fermented, or broken down, by bacteria.

The thigh bone was 75 cm (30 in) long and very strong.

Large, oval bony plates were surrounded by smaller plates, together giving effective protection.

Saltasaurus was up to 12.8 m (42 ft) long.

Saltasaurus

It did not have toes or claws on its front feet.

CERAPODS

These plant-eaters had beak-like jaws for snapping stems and twigs. Cerapods also had a thicker coating, called enamel, on the insides of their lower front teeth. As a result, their teeth wore away unevenly during chewing, making sharp ridges that were perfect for mushing plants.

The cerapods can be divided into the ornithopods (from the ancient Greek for "bird feet") and the marginocephalians ("fringed heads").

The ornithopods take their name from their usually three-toed feet, which were a little like those of modern birds. Smaller, earlier members of the group walked on their back legs, but heavier, later ornithopods usually walked on all fours. These effective plant-eaters had several rows of grinding teeth as well as cheek pouches for holding food. The ornithopods included the hypsilophodonts, iguanodonts, and hadrosaurs.

The marginocephalian dinosaurs had a bony shelf at the back of their skull, which may have been a feature that attracted a mate. The marginocephalians are divided into two groups: the ceratopsians ("horned faces") and the pachycephalosaurs ("thick-headed lizards"). All ceratopsians had a large beak. Later members of the group had splendid horns and neck frills. The pachycephalosaurs had thick, often domed, skulls.

The large-nosed ornithopod *Altirhinus* ran on its two back legs, but may have walked on all fours when feeding on low plants.

Cerapod Beaks

The cerapods were ornithischian ("bird-hipped") dinosaurs, with hip bones that looked like those of birds. Ornithischians had an extra bone at the front of their lower jaw, helping to form a beak. Both upper and lower jaws were covered in hard, horny keratin, which is also found in claws.

Like other ornithischians, the ceratopsian *Styracosaurus* had an extra bone in its jaw, called the predentary.

In Cretaceous North America, a startled *Stygimoloch* pachycephalosaur (left), runs away from a *Pectinodon* theropod.

Little *Hypsilophodon*'s best protection was to stick with its herd—and run fast when necessary.

HYPSILOPHODONTS

These small, early cerapods ran fast on their long back legs, using their stiff tail for balance. Since _Hypsilophodon_ were short, they fed on low-growing plants, using their hard, pointed beaks for snapping shoots and roots, as well as perhaps catching insects and other little creatures. Large eyes helped _Hypsilophodon_ watch for predators while they ate.

Hypsilophodon teeth sharpened themselves. Their upper teeth curved inwards, while their lower teeth curved outward. As the two sets of teeth rubbed against each other during chewing, sharp ridges were formed. This process slowly wore the teeth right down, so new teeth moved, slowly and steadily, from the back of the mouth to replace them. As well as having 28 to 30 of these plant-grinding teeth, _Hypsilophodon_ had five pointed teeth at the front of their upper jaw for clipping off twigs.

The bodies of many _Hypsilophodon_ have been found close together, so they may have lived in large herds, grazing in Cretaceous forests and woodland like modern deer. When one member of the herd smelled, saw, or heard an approaching predator, they would have alerted the whole group with a noise or sudden movement. Then the herd could run for safety, moving faster than the heavier theropods, such as _Neovenator_, that were their predators.

Hypsilophodon had five fingers on each hand and, unlike later ornithopods, four toes on each foot.

Family:	Hypsilophodontidae
Range:	Europe
Time Period:	Early Cretaceous, 130–125 million years ago
Size Range:	1.5–1.8 m (5–6 ft) long

Hypsilophodon

DINOSAUR SENSES

Sight, smell, and hearing were important senses for dinosaurs, enabling them to find food, escape predators, and get a mate. Paleontologists can study these senses by looking at the shape of dinosaurs' skull bones, such as the eye sockets. Less is known about dinosaurs' senses of taste and touch, because tongues and nerves have not been fossilized.

Bistahieversor

There were important differences between the senses of meat-eaters and plant-eaters. Meat-eaters had big, forward-facing eyes that helped them see prey. Having two forward-facing eyes enables the eyes to work together to judge how far away prey is, as well as how fast it is moving. In contrast, plant-eaters often had smaller eyes, which were positioned on the sides of their head so they could watch all around for approaching predators. Some meat-eaters, including tyrannosaurs, also had better senses of smell than plant-eaters, so they could sniff out prey.

Dinosaurs had ear holes that were probably not surrounded by fleshy outer ears like those of humans or dogs.

Tyrannosaurus

Tyrannosaurus's sense of smell was as powerful as a modern bloodhound's.

Like other meat-eaters, tyrannosaurs had forward-facing eyes, which could probably see prey up to 6 km (3.7 miles) away.

Its tongue was simple, flat, and attached to the floor of the mouth, so *Tyrannosaurus* could not stick out its tongue like a lizard does.

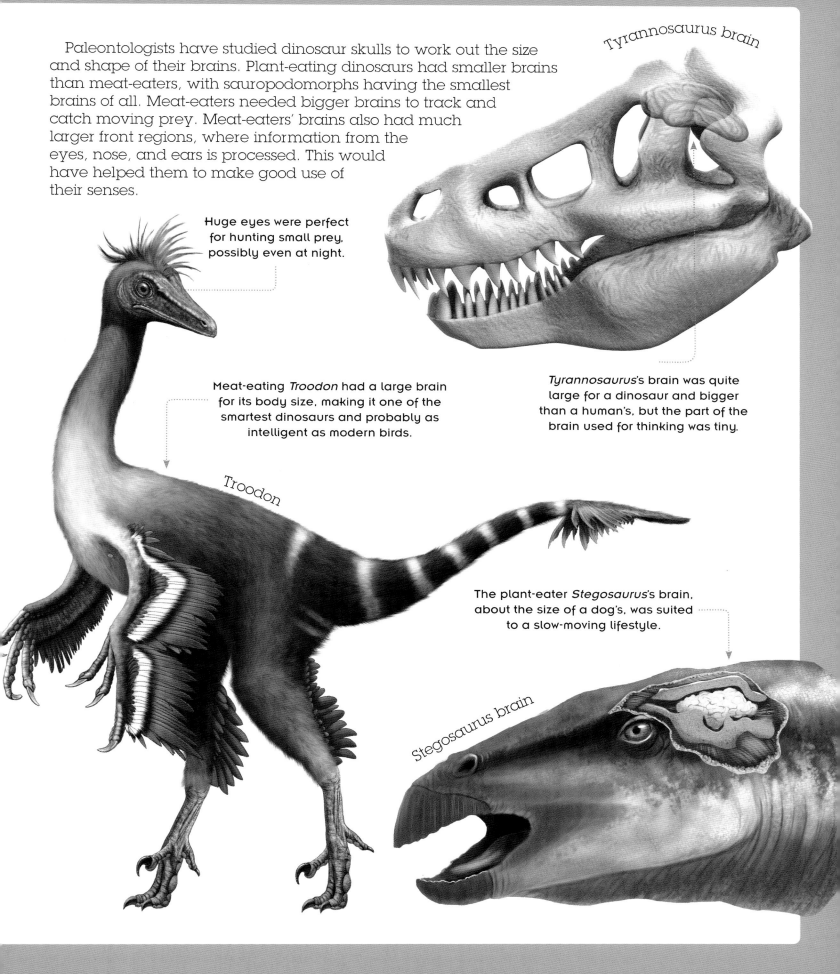

Paleontologists have studied dinosaur skulls to work out the size and shape of their brains. Plant-eating dinosaurs had smaller brains than meat-eaters, with sauropodomorphs having the smallest brains of all. Meat-eaters needed bigger brains to track and catch moving prey. Meat-eaters' brains also had much larger front regions, where information from the eyes, nose, and ears is processed. This would have helped them to make good use of their senses.

Tyrannosaurus brain

Huge eyes were perfect for hunting small prey, possibly even at night.

Meat-eating *Troodon* had a large brain for its body size, making it one of the smartest dinosaurs and probably as intelligent as modern birds.

Tyrannosaurus's brain was quite large for a dinosaur and bigger than a human's, but the part of the brain used for thinking was tiny.

Troodon

The plant-eater *Stegosaurus*'s brain, about the size of a dog's, was suited to a slow-moving lifestyle.

Stegosaurus brain

IGUANODONTS

Unlike most animals, iguanodonts could walk as easily on two legs as on four. When these plant-eaters needed to move fast, they sprinted on their back legs. As an iguanodont got older and heavier, it spent more time wandering slowly on all fours. Some iguanodonts had a sharp thumb spike, which they could use to stab theropod predators.

Iguanodont hands were suited both to walking and to holding food. The second, third, and fourth fingers were strong and stiff to take the dinosaur's weight. The thumb and its spike, which could have been used to open fruit, were held off the ground while walking. The fifth finger was long and bendy, to help with holding fruit or branches.

The Iguanodontidae family is named after the *Iguanodon* genus, which was itself named in 1825 by the English paleontologist Gideon Mantell, after his wife had found its fossil. *Iguanodon* was only the second species of dinosaur, after the theropod *Megalosaurus*, to be given a scientific name. Mantell chose to name *Iguanodon* after the ancient Greek for "iguana tooth" because its teeth were similar to those of modern iguanas, a group of plant-eating lizards. This was also a clue to Mantell that dinosaurs were reptiles, a fact that was unknown at the time.

The three middle toes of an *Iguanodon*'s feet had blunt, hard claws like a horse's hooves.

Family:	Iguanodontidae
Range:	Europe and Africa
Time Period:	Early Cretaceous, 140–112 million years ago
Size Range:	8–13 m (26–43 ft) long

Barilium

Iguanodon

In Cretaceous England, a pack of *Aristosuchus* risks an attack on a grazing *Iguanodon*, which spears one with its thumb spike.

HADROSAURS

Often called duck-billed dinosaurs, hadrosaurs had long, flattened snouts that looked a little like a duck's beak. These were ideal for snapping off tough twigs and leaves. Some hadrosaurs had a bony crest on their head. Hadrosaurs usually walked on four legs, but could rear up on their hind legs to reach high branches.

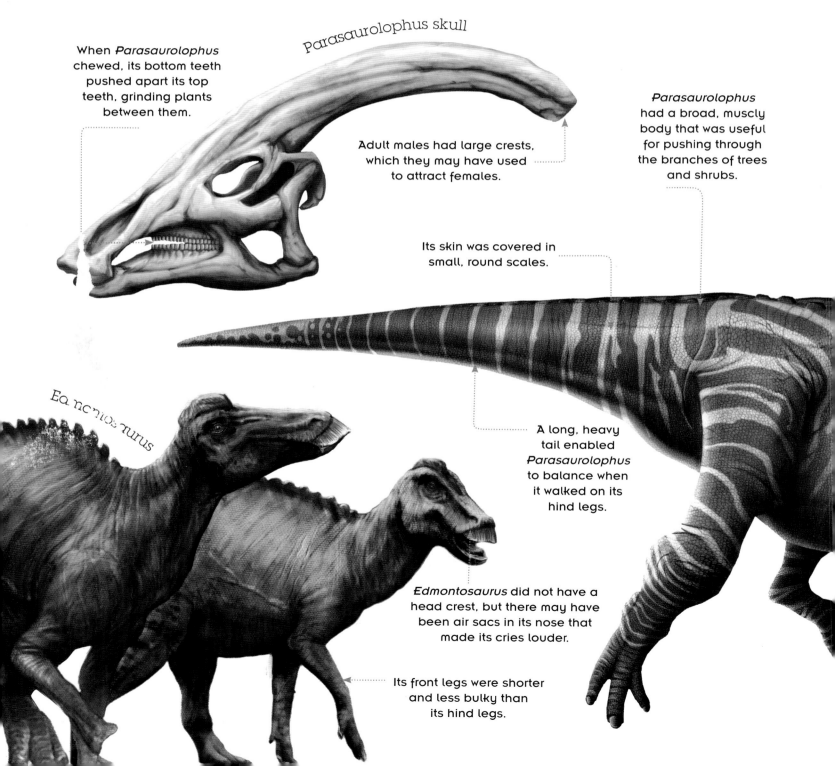

Parasaurolophus skull

When *Parasaurolophus* chewed, its bottom teeth pushed apart its top teeth, grinding plants between them.

Adult males had large crests, which they may have used to attract females.

Parasaurolophus had a broad, muscly body that was useful for pushing through the branches of trees and shrubs.

Its skin was covered in small, round scales.

A long, heavy tail enabled *Parasaurolophus* to balance when it walked on its hind legs.

Edmontosaurus

Edmontosaurus did not have a head crest, but there may have been air sacs in its nose that made its cries louder.

Its front legs were shorter and less bulky than its hind legs.

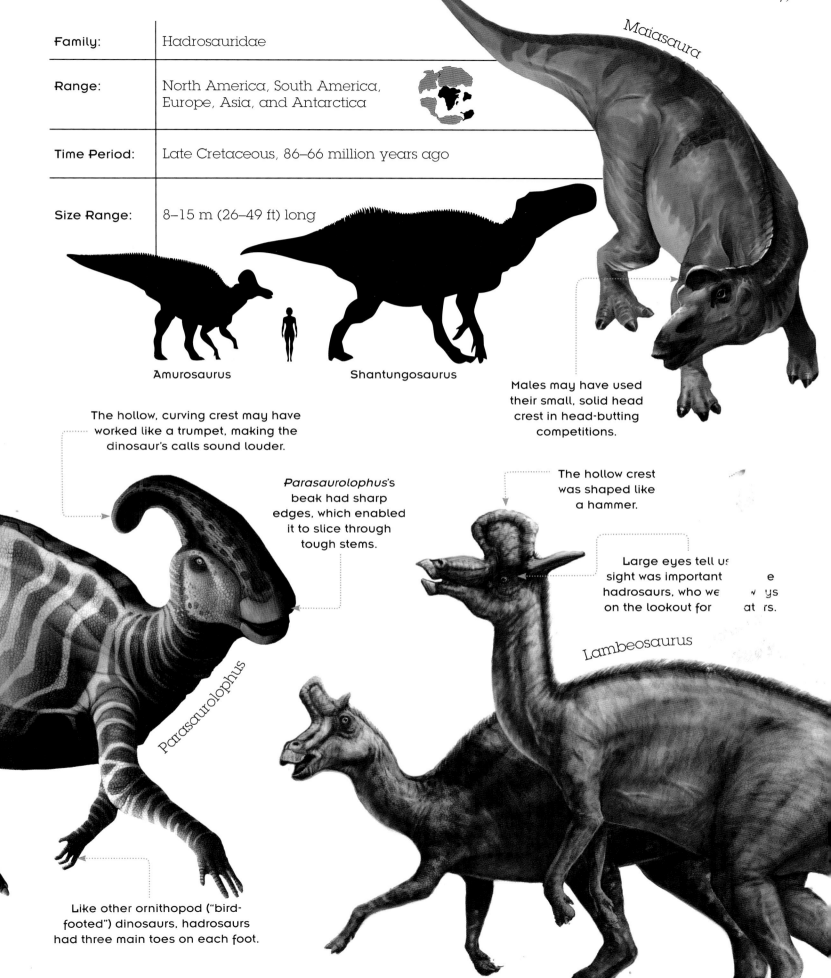

Family:	Hadrosauridae
Range:	North America, South America, Europe, Asia, and Antarctica
Time Period:	Late Cretaceous, 86–66 million years ago
Size Range:	8–15 m (26–49 ft) long

Amurosaurus

Shantungosaurus

Maiasaura

Males may have used their small, solid head crest in head-butting competitions.

The hollow, curving crest may have worked like a trumpet, making the dinosaur's calls sound louder.

Parasaurolophus's beak had sharp edges, which enabled it to slice through tough stems.

The hollow crest was shaped like a hammer.

Large eyes tell us sight was important   e hadrosaurs, who we   ys on the lookout for   rs.

Lambeosaurus

Parasaurolophus

Like other ornithopod ("bird-footed") dinosaurs, hadrosaurs had three main toes on each foot.

DINOSAUR COMMUNICATION

By making sounds or using body language, dinosaurs could warn each other about threats, frighten off attackers, and attract a mate. Paleontologists base their ideas about dinosaur communication on the way that modern birds and reptiles behave. Just like today's animals, dinosaurs would have used a range of calls and displays to "talk."

Rather than roaring like a lion, dinosaurs may have made low grunting, rumbling, and booming sounds with their mouths closed. Such sounds, made by pushing air up through the throat, are used by birds and reptiles today. Like these modern animals, dinosaurs may have been capable of a range of different sounds, from alarms to mating calls. Studies on the bones around dinosaur ears have shown they were probably good at hearing low sounds. Low sounds travel long distances, so they could be heard by a scattered herd, or by distant females at mating time.

The diplodocid *Apatosaurus* could have cracked its tail like a whip to frighten away predators, making a noise as loud as a cannon being fired.

This hadrosaur might have blown air through its hollow nose crest, making its honking calls louder.

Olorotitan

Apatosaurus

The double crest on meat-eater *Dilophosaurus's* head was too weak to be used in battles, so it may have been a feature that attracted a mate.

Dilophosaurus

Many dinosaurs have strangely shaped and unusually large body parts—including head crests, neck frills, back humps, and domed skulls—that seem to have no useful purpose. Many modern reptiles and birds have similar features, such as the neck frill of the frilled lizard and the long tail of the peacock. Among modern animals, these body parts are displayed while strutting or posing, with the aim of attracting a mate or driving away rivals. It is likely that some dinosaurs did the same, with the largest body parts having the most success.

This theropod may have shown off its hump to warn other males to stay out of its territory.

Concavenator

A *Khaan* theropod might have displayed its large tail when trying to attract a female.

Khaan mating display

Like modern peahens, the female may have chosen her mate by his healthy-looking feathers and bold display.

Unlike their short-armed parents, young *Psittacosauruses* probably walked on all fours as they looked for shoots and seeds on the forest floor.

PSITTACOSAURS

These ceratopsians were named psittacosaurs, meaning "parrot lizards," because of the shape of their skull and beak. Psittacosaurs' big, strong beaks were suited to crushing seeds, like those of parrots. These dinosaurs also had almost round, parrot-like skulls. Unlike later, larger ceratopsians, psittacosaurs walked on two legs, rather than four, as adults.

Psittacosaurs could slide their bottom jaw forward and backward. If the bottom jaw was pulled back, so it was inside the top jaw, it could work like a hinged nutcracker, splitting open nuts and hard seeds. If the bottom jaw was pushed forward, so it lined up with the top jaw, it could snip off leaves and twigs. Unlike later ceratopsians, psittacosaurs did not have teeth suited to chewing up tough plant material. Instead, these dinosaurs swallowed stones, which ground up plants inside their stomach.

The skin of psittacosaurs was covered in scales. Scientists have studied small structures in their fossilized skin to work out what shade it was. They think that psittacosaurs were brown with a paler belly, as well as having some spots and stripes on their legs. This dappled skin would have been excellent camouflage in forests, where sunlight falls in stripes and patches through the leaves.

On *Psittacosaurus*'s tail was a fringe of long bristles, which may have been used for displays at mating time.

Family:	Psittacosauridae
Range:	Asia 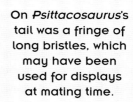
Time Period:	Early Cretaceous, 126–101 million years ago
Size Range:	1.4–2 m (4.6–6.6 ft) long

Psittacosaurus
ordosensis

Psittacosaurus
sibericus

PROTOCERATOPSIANS

These early ceratopsians were littler and had smaller bony frills and horns than later members of their group. Protoceratopsians walked on all fours, probably moving quite slowly on their short legs. They used their hooked beaks for plucking plants, then munched using their dozens of teeth. Their jaws were large and strong, giving them a powerful bite and chew.

The shape and size of the bones around protoceratopsians' eyes suggest that many of them had big eyes. Large eyes are common both in animals that are predators, when they are used for watching prey, and in animals that are active at night, when they help with seeing in dim light. Since protoceratopsians' jaws and teeth tell us they were definitely plant-eaters, some paleontologists think they may have been nocturnal, or active at night. Protoceratopsians are believed to have lived in hot deserts, so being nocturnal would have been a good way to avoid the burning sun. Other paleontologists wonder if protoceratopsians were active for a few hours, then slept for a few hours, throughout the day and night, like modern hamsters.

Although protoceratopsians did not have fully formed horns on their faces, they did have bumps on their snouts.

Males had bigger bumps than females, so these may have been features that males showed off to females at mating time.

Some *Protoceratops* had very large neck frills, while others had a smaller one. Dinosaurs with larger frills may have attracted more mates.

Family:	Protoceratopsidae
Range:	Asia
Time Period:	Late Cretaceous, 85–70.6 million years ago
Size Range:	1.5–2 m (5–6.6 ft) long

Graciliceratops

Protoceratops

Protoceratops mothers laid their eggs carefully in circular nests, then may have watched over them till they hatched.

CERATOPSIANS

Ceratopsian skulls were decorated with sharp horns on the brows or noses, as well as frills that extended over the animal's neck. These plant-eaters wandered on four legs, probably in large herds like modern buffalo. Ceratopsians always had to be on the lookout for hungry tyrannosaurs, but their large size protected them from all but the fiercest attacks.

The edge of the frill was decorated with shorter horns and knobs.

Centrosaurus

Weighing up to 12 tonnes (13 US tons), *Triceratops* could have made deadly charges at predators, like a modern rhino.

Horns above the eyes were a distinguishing feature that would have helped a *Centrosaurus* to recognize other members of its species.

Chasmosaurus

Triceratops

Chasmosaurus's exceptionally long frill was shield-shaped.

Its skin was covered in small scales, with larger bony plates, called scutes, on its underside.

Short toes were protected by hoof-like claws.

Family:	Ceratopsidae
Range:	North America and Asia
Time Period:	Late Cretaceous, 83–66 million years ago
Size Range:	4.5–9 m (15–30 ft) long

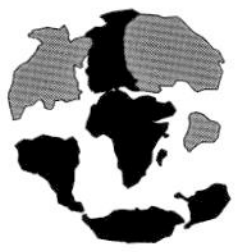

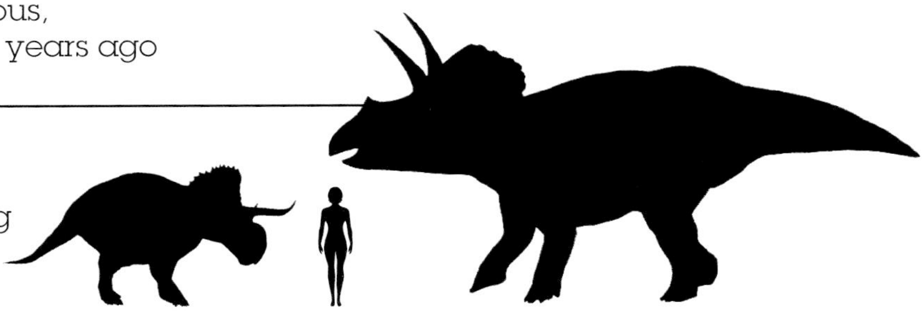

Nasutoceratops

Eotriceratops

The frill may have defended the neck from bites, but it was more likely a feature that attracted a mate.

Triceratops (meaning "three-horned face") had two horns on its brow, up to 1 m (3.3 ft) long, and one on its nose.

Four to six bone spikes extended from *Styracosaurus*'s neck frill.

A 60-cm (2-ft) nose horn was probably used in battles over mates and leadership with other members of the herd.

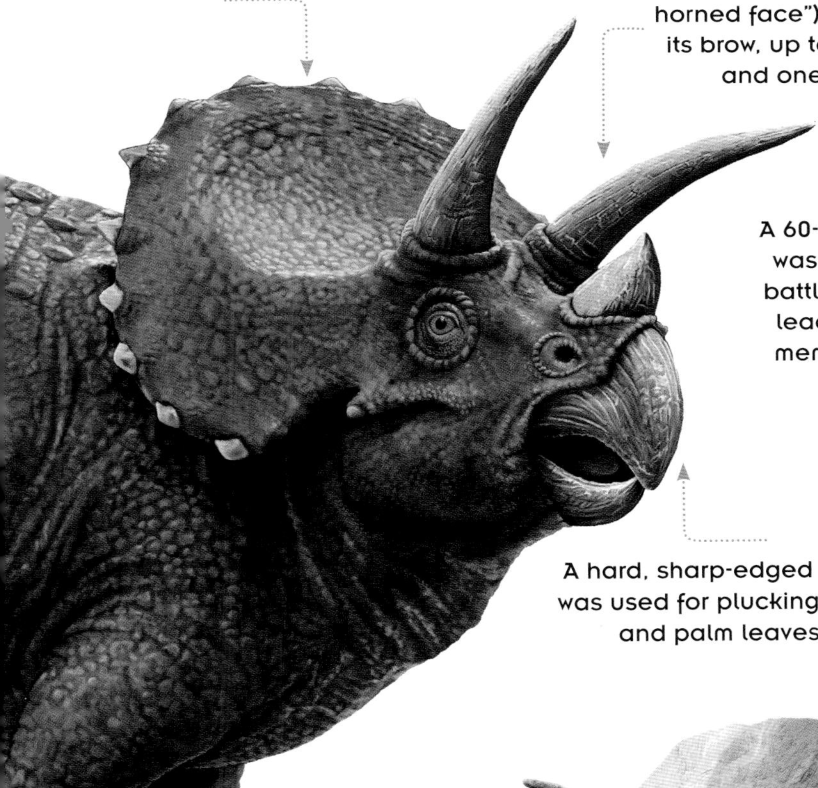

A hard, sharp-edged beak was used for plucking ferns and palm leaves.

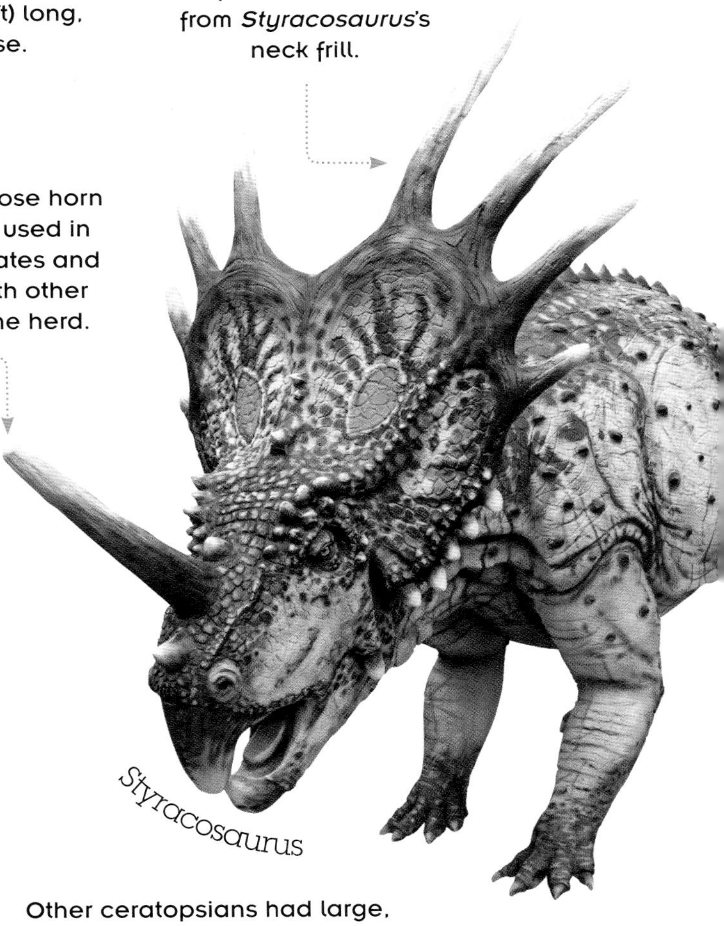

Styracosaurus

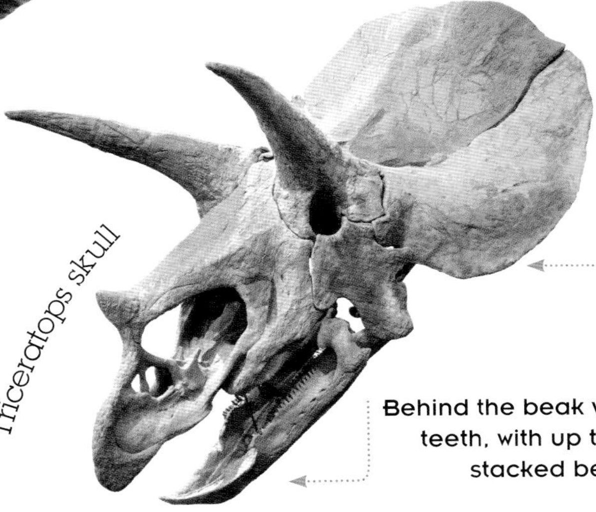

Triceratops skull

Other ceratopsians had large, skin-covered holes in their frill bones that made them lighter, but a *Triceratops* frill was solid.

Behind the beak were 36 to 40 plant-mashing teeth, with up to 760 replacement teeth stacked below the ones in use.

Two male *Prenocephales* ram each other with their hard, spiked skulls.

PACHYCEPHALOSAURS

Pachycephalosaurs had very thick, unusually shaped skulls. Some had domed or wedge-shaped skulls, while others—perhaps females or young dinosaurs that were not fully grown—had strangely flat tops to their heads. The domes were decorated by bumps and spikes. Walking on their back legs, pachycephalosaurs ate leaves, roots, and possibly small animals.

Many paleontologists think that pachycephalosaurs used their very strong skulls in head-butting competitions. Males may have competed with each other for females, leadership, or the best feeding areas. Modern mountain goats ram each other in this way. Some pachycephalosaur skulls show damage that could have been done during such a fight.

Pachycephalosaurs had large eyes, so they are likely to have had good eyesight. The very front area of their brain, where smells are analyzed, was also large. This suggests that these dinosaurs were well suited to both finding food and keeping watch for predators such as *Tyrannosaurus*.

The teeth at the front of pachycephalosaurs' mouths were sharp and pointed, like those of a meat-eating dinosaur. Their back teeth were broad and leaf-shaped, making them good for chewing leaves. This mix of teeth, as well as pachycephalosaurs' very good senses, have made paleontologists wonder if these dinosaurs were omnivores, eating insects and other small animals as well as plants.

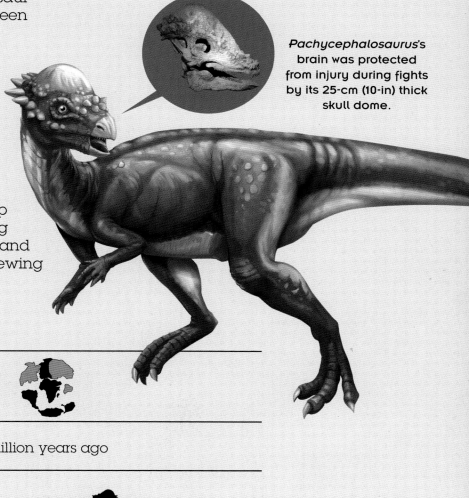

Pachycephalosaurus's brain was protected from injury during fights by its 25-cm (10-in) thick skull dome.

Family:	Pachycephalosauridae
Range:	North America and Asia
Time Period:	Late Cretaceous, 90–66 million years ago
Size Range:	2–4.5 m (6.6–15 ft) long

Foraminacephale   Pachycephalosaurus

THYREOPHORANS

These plant-eating dinosaurs had superb protection against fierce meat-eaters. Thyreophorans means "shield bearers" in ancient Greek. While early thyreophorans just had a covering of bony plates, their later relatives had thick plates, tall spikes, or heavy tail clubs.

The earliest members of this group, such as *Scutellosaurus*, evolved in the early Jurassic Period. They were small and light enough to walk on their back legs. Their little bony plates would have protected them against small predators but would not have saved their lives from the large meat-eating dinosaurs that were evolving alongside them.

After a few more million years, better-protected thyreophorans, such as *Scelidosaurus*, evolved. These dinosaurs were larger and had bigger bony plates. Like their later relatives, their great weight meant they walked slowly on all fours.

By the middle Jurassic Period, thyreophorans had split into two subgroups: stegosaurians (meaning "covered lizards") and ankylosaurians (meaning "stiff lizards"). The stegosaurians had rows of spikes or plates running down their backs, as well as spiked tails. The ankylosaurians had bodies rather like army tanks, protected by almost solid plates of bone.

Living in the early Cretaceous Period, ankylosaurs like *Gastonia* had sacrificed speed and agility for a large and heavily protected body.

Thyreophoran Legs

Apart from early thyreophorans, these dinosaurs had thick legs and broad feet. Their front legs were usually much shorter than their back legs. All this suggests thyreophorans were slow walkers and awkward runners. Thyreophorans were ornithischian ("bird-hipped") dinosaurs.

Having short front legs meant that *Mymoorapelta* had a rounded back and held its tail above the ground.

An ankylosaur, named *Zuul* after a monster from the 1984 film *Ghostbusters*, uses its tail club to fend off a *Daspletosaurus*.

SCALES, SCUTES, AND SPIKES

Although some meat-eating dinosaurs had feathers, most dinosaurs had skin covered by scales. The thyreophorans also had bigger, harder coverings called scutes, which gave them greater protection than scales. Some had scutes shaped into tall plates or sharp spikes, which may have been weapons or just for decoration.

Scales are small, hard plates that grow from the top layer of an animal's skin to protect it from drying out or being damaged. Scales are made of keratin, the same material as in human nails. Like the scales of modern snakes, dinosaur scales were a range of shapes and sizes. They often had smaller scales on body parts that needed to move easily, such as legs, and larger scales on areas, such as the soles of the feet, that got more wear.

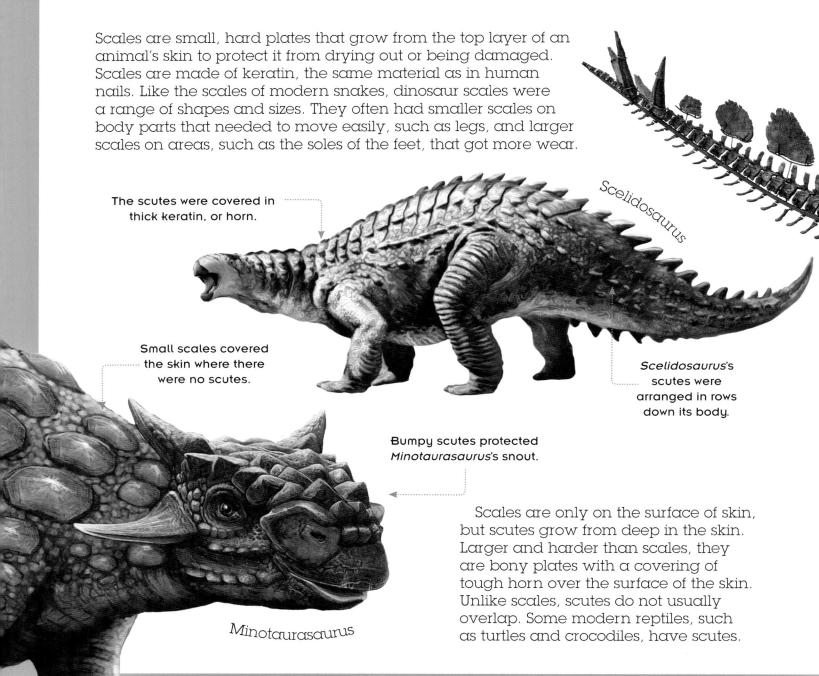

The scutes were covered in thick keratin, or horn.

Small scales covered the skin where there were no scutes.

Scelidosaurus

Scelidosaurus's scutes were arranged in rows down its body.

Bumpy scutes protected *Minotaurasaurus*'s snout.

Minotaurasaurus

Scales are only on the surface of skin, but scutes grow from deep in the skin. Larger and harder than scales, they are bony plates with a covering of tough horn over the surface of the skin. Unlike scales, scutes do not usually overlap. Some modern reptiles, such as turtles and crocodiles, have scutes.

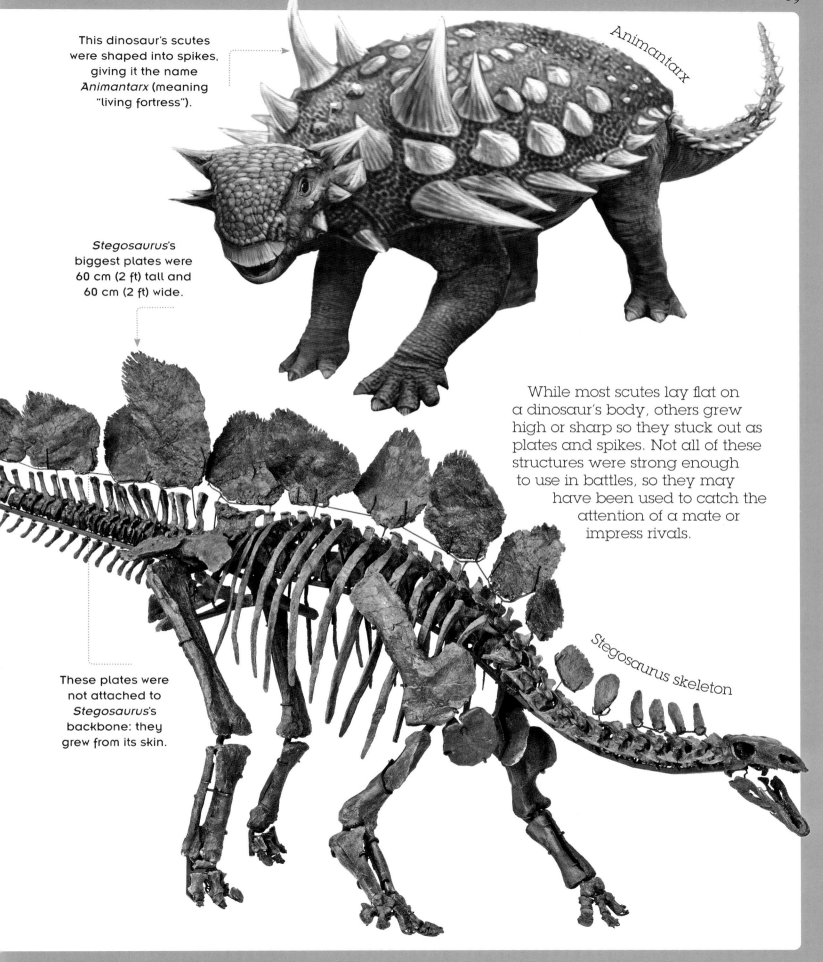

This dinosaur's scutes were shaped into spikes, giving it the name *Animantarx* (meaning "living fortress").

Animantarx

Stegosaurus's biggest plates were 60 cm (2 ft) tall and 60 cm (2 ft) wide.

While most scutes lay flat on a dinosaur's body, others grew high or sharp so they stuck out as plates and spikes. Not all of these structures were strong enough to use in battles, so they may have been used to catch the attention of a mate or impress rivals.

Stegosaurus skeleton

These plates were not attached to *Stegosaurus*'s backbone: they grew from its skin.

Its fairly light scutes and long back legs meant *Scutellosaurus* could move fast, but perhaps not fast enough to escape *Dilophosaurus*.

SCUTELLOSAURS

The earliest and smallest of the thyreophorans, *Scutellosaurus* ran fast on its two back legs. When feeding, it could also put down its short "arms." *Scutellosaurus*'s name means "little-shielded lizard." It had simple scutes along its neck and back, as well as a long tail to balance the extra weight of its body.

Scutellosaurus had hundreds of scutes, arranged in rows along its neck, back, and sides. Depending on where they were on the body, the scutes were different sizes and shapes, some long and flat and others triangular with a high ridge, like smaller versions of the tall plates found on later thyreophorans.

Its small scutes enabled *Scutellosaurus* to still bend and twist, but also gave some protection against the teeth and claws of meat-eaters its own size. In *Scutellosaurus*'s part of North America, these included the small theropod *Kayentavenator*.

Yet larger theropods, with bigger jaws, were evolving in the region, including the 3-m (10-ft) long *Ceolophysis* and, even more dangerous, the 7-m (23-ft) long *Dilophosaurus*. Running away was *Scutellosaurus*'s only strategy against these hefty, larger-toothed predators.

Using its leaf-shaped, rough-edged teeth, *Scutellosaurus* clipped leaves from low branches. The *Scutellosaurus* teeth found so far by paleontologists are not worn away, which suggests that it did not chew its food before swallowing.

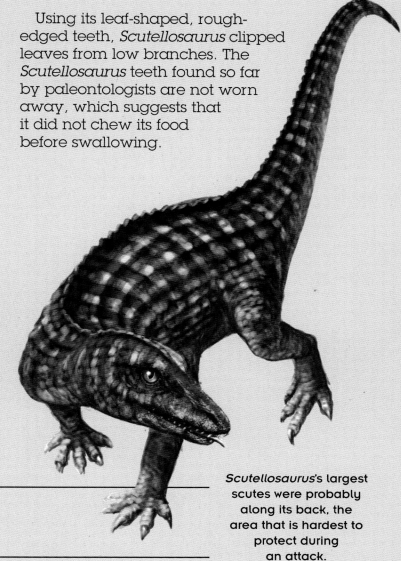

Scutellosaurus's largest scutes were probably along its back, the area that is hardest to protect during an attack.

Family:	Scutellosauridae
Range:	North America
Time Period:	Early Jurassic, 196 million years ago
Size Range:	1.2 m (3.9 ft) long

Scutellosaurus

EMAUSAURS

With its spiky scutes, *Emausaurus* was more heavily protected than earlier thyreophorans. It was also bigger and weightier. As an adult, *Emausaurus* probably moved on all fours, but it may have walked on its back legs while still a young dinosaur, before it had reached its full size and weight. As *Emausaurus* wandered, it grazed on low shrubs and ferns.

Emausaurus was named after Ernst Moritz Arndt University (EMAU), whose students helped preserve its fossils, which were found in northern Germany in the 1960s. The fossils were discovered by workmen, who contacted the university. They did not discover a complete skeleton, just bits of one dinosaur's skull, jaws, legs, and feet, as well as three cone-shaped scutes and one tall, spiky scute.

Based only on these fossils, paleontologists have had to piece together what they think *Emausaurus* looked like, taking some ideas from the body of a dinosaur they think is a close relative: *Scelidosaurus*. After considering the size of *Emausaurus*'s bones, paleontologists think an adult would have weighed around 240 kg (530 lb), about three times the weight of an average man.

Many other fossils from the early Jurassic Period have been found in the same area as *Emausaurus*, including land animals such as insects and sauropodomorph dinosaurs, and sea creatures from fish to swimming reptiles. The collection suggests this part of Germany was a seashore during the Jurassic Period.

Emausaurus had a long, almost triangular-shaped skull with a pointed snout.

Genus:	Emausaurus
Range:	Europe
Time Period:	Early Jurassic, 181 million years ago
Size Range:	3–4 m (9.8–13 ft) long

Emausaurus

Emausaurus munches on ferns, while Jurassic insects resembling modern grasshoppers, beetles, and dragonflies hop, scuttle, and fly past.

In Jurassic England, *Scelidosaurus* was at risk from meat-eaters such as the sharp-toothed *Megalosaurus*, which reached 9 m (29.5 ft) long.

SCELIDOSAURS

Scelidosaurus's face, neck, back, and tail were protected by hundreds of scutes, both large and small, round and oval, spiked and flat. These scutes were strong enough to snap the teeth of its enemies. Fossils of this dinosaur have only ever been found around Charmouth on the south coast of England, with the first discovery in 1858.

Scelidosaurus's scutes were in parallel rows. The larger scutes had a high ridge that stuck out from the body, making it tricky for a predator to get a grip on *Scelidosaurus*'s flesh with its jaws or claws. Some scutes may also have had horns or spikes. Between the bony scutes, the skin was protected by small scales.

Scelidosaurus fed on leaves up to 1 m (3.3 ft) above the ground, snipping them off with its leaf-shaped teeth. This dinosaur was not a good chewer, as its jaws were able to move only up and down. Food was probably mashed a little between the upper and lower teeth, then swallowed.

In *Scelidosaurus*'s large stomach, food may have been broken down by tiny bacteria that lived there naturally. Today, this is how cows and some other large plant-eaters get the goodness from the plants they eat.

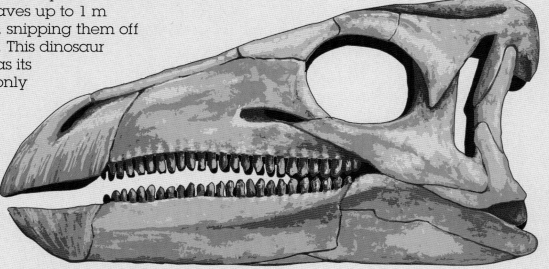

Family:	Scelidosauridae
Range:	Europe
Time Period:	Early Jurassic, 197–183 million years ago
Size Range:	3–4 m (9.8–13 ft) long

Scelidosaurus

In addition to its nostrils and eye sockets, *Scelidosaurus* had other openings in its skull, in front of and behind its eyes, which kept the skull lightweight. Later thyreophorans had stronger skulls without these openings.

DINOSAUR SPEED

The fastest dinosaurs could probably have run faster than a human athlete. Yet the slowest dinosaurs might easily have been outrun by a child. Paleontologists base their guesses about dinosaur speed on studies of their footprints and body shapes, as well as on the speeds of modern animals.

A series of dinosaur footprints, called a trackway, can give clues about how fast the animal was walking or running. To make guesses about speed, paleontologists use measurements of the size and depth of the footprints, as well as the distance between them. They work out which dinosaur may have made the prints by comparing features such as the number of toes with dinosaur bones found in the region. The fastest running speed measured from any trackway is about 43 km (26.7 miles) per hour, a little faster than the best human sprinters. The trackway was made by a medium-sized theropod.

A sauropod has left deep, neat footprints as it walked slowly.

The best trackways were left in soft mud after the tide had gone out.

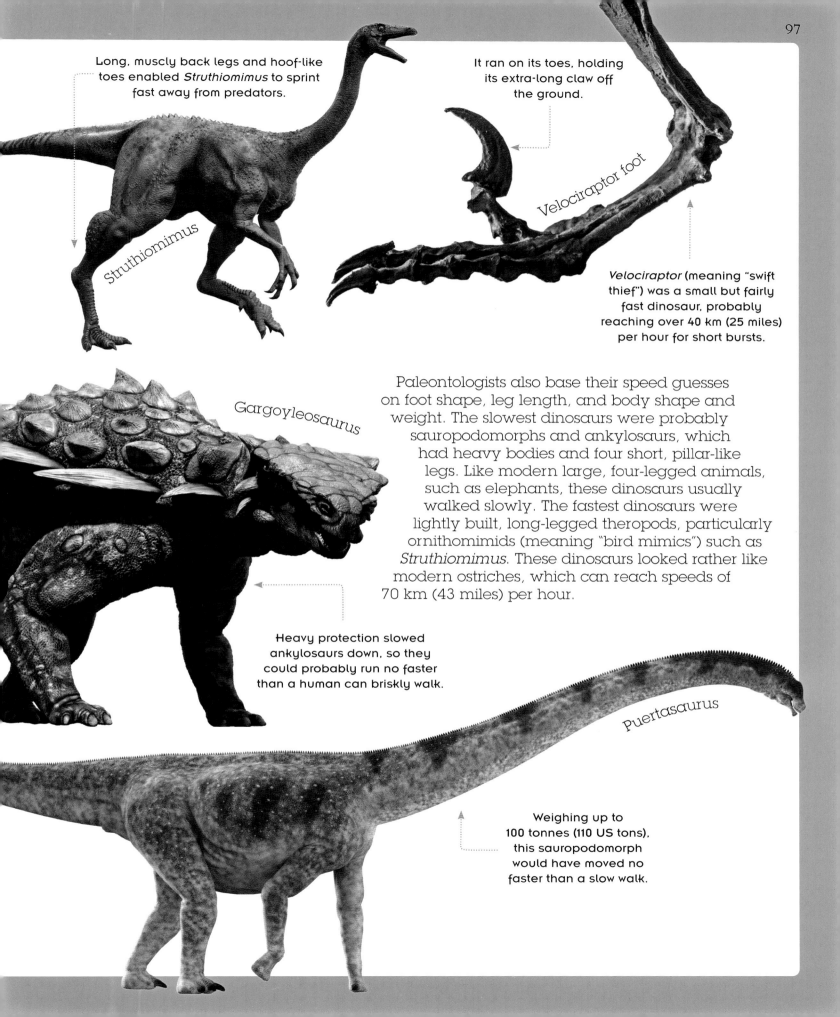

Long, muscly back legs and hoof-like toes enabled *Struthiomimus* to sprint fast away from predators.

It ran on its toes, holding its extra-long claw off the ground.

Velociraptor foot

Struthiomimus

Velociraptor (meaning "swift thief") was a small but fairly fast dinosaur, probably reaching over 40 km (25 miles) per hour for short bursts.

Gargoyleosaurus

Paleontologists also base their speed guesses on foot shape, leg length, and body shape and weight. The slowest dinosaurs were probably sauropodomorphs and ankylosaurs, which had heavy bodies and four short, pillar-like legs. Like modern large, four-legged animals, such as elephants, these dinosaurs usually walked slowly. The fastest dinosaurs were lightly built, long-legged theropods, particularly ornithomimids (meaning "bird mimics") such as *Struthiomimus*. These dinosaurs looked rather like modern ostriches, which can reach speeds of 70 km (43 miles) per hour.

Heavy protection slowed ankylosaurs down, so they could probably run no faster than a human can briskly walk.

Puertasaurus

Weighing up to 100 tonnes (110 US tons), this sauropodomorph would have moved no faster than a slow walk.

HUAYANGOSAURS

The huayangosaurs were a family of early stegosaurians. They were much smaller than later stegosaurians, but like their relatives they had spiked tails and tall plates down their backs. Huayangosaurs walked on four legs as they searched for low-growing plants to snip off with their horn-covered beak.

The member of the family that is best known from fossils is *Huayangosaurus*. It had two rows of tall plates and spikes along its neck, back, and tail. These plates were smaller than those of later stegosaurs. The spiky plates above the hips were longest, perhaps to protect against attacks from above on this fairly short dinosaur. *Huayangosaurus* also had two long shoulder spikes. These might have been useful during an attack, but such impressive features could also have been displayed to attract a mate. Smaller scutes protected *Huayangosaurus*'s sides.

The tip of *Huayangosaurus*'s tail had a small club, while toward the end were two pairs of spikes forming a weapon known as a thagomizer. By thrashing and flicking their tails, these dinosaurs could have used thagomizers as a powerful defensive weapon. The name "thagomizer" was made up for these weapons in 1982, by Gary Larson in his funny *The Far Side* cartoons. Paleontologists liked the name and started to use it.

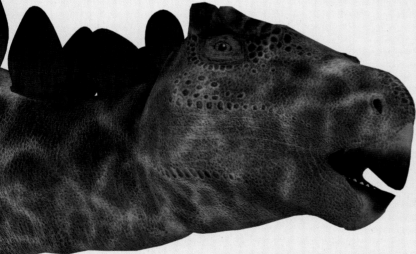

These dinosaurs pulled off leaves and twigs using their hard-edged beaks, with help from 14 spade-like teeth at the front of their top jaw.

Family:	Huayangosauridae
Range:	Europe and Asia
Time Period:	Middle Jurassic to early Cretaceous, 165–121 million years ago
Size Range:	4–5 m (13–16.4 ft) long

Regnosaurus   Chungkingosaurus

Huayangosaurus lived in what is now China's Huayang province, which was rich with plant and animal life due to its lakes and rivers.

Stegosaurs

Stegosaurs had thin plates or spikes along the top of their neck, back, and tail, but these would have been little help in a battle. Without scutes on their sides, stegosaurs' only real security was offered by their thagomizer. It is possible that stegosaurs' plates were no longer for protection at all, but were just decoration to attract a mate.

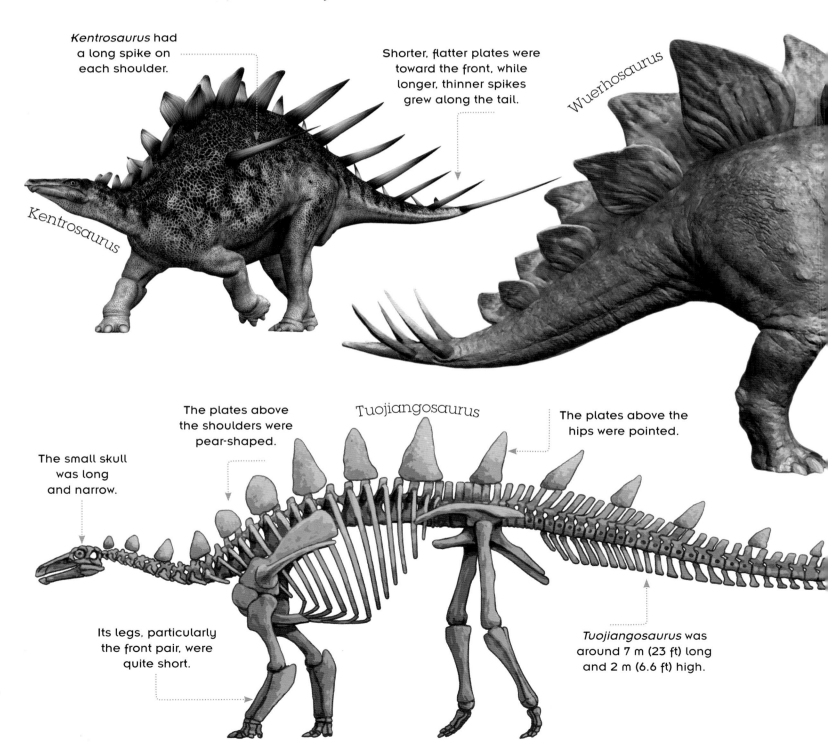

Kentrosaurus had a long spike on each shoulder.

Shorter, flatter plates were toward the front, while longer, thinner spikes grew along the tail.

Wuerhosaurus

Kentrosaurus

Tuojiangosaurus

The plates above the shoulders were pear-shaped.

The plates above the hips were pointed.

The small skull was long and narrow.

Its legs, particularly the front pair, were quite short.

Tuojiangosaurus was around 7 m (23 ft) long and 2 m (6.6 ft) high.

The biggest plates were 60 cm (24 in) tall.

Stegosaurus

It had two rows of kite-shaped plates.

Wuerhosaurus had a broad belly to hold lots of leaves as they were slowly digested.

Stegosaurus grew up to 9 m (29.5 m) long.

The tail spikes were 60–90 cm (2–3 ft) long.

Stegosaurus thagomizer

A long neck and narrow head enabled it to reach the best parts of plants.

Injuries to *Stegosaurus* tails suggests that these dinosaurs used their thagomizers in combat.

The thagomizer had two pairs of strong, sharp spikes.

Family:	Stegosauridae	
Range:	North America, Europe, Asia, and Africa	
Time Period:	Middle Jurassic to early Cretaceous, 165–125 million years ago	
Size Range:	5–10 m (16.4–32.8 ft) long	

Yingshanosaurus

Dacentrurus

During an attack by *Acrocanthosaurus*, *Borealopelta* needs to protect its softer, weaker belly.

NODOSAURS

Nodosaurs (meaning "knobbed lizards") were a family of ankylosaurians. Like other ankylosaurians, they were heavily shielded, with scute-covered bodies and spear-like spikes jutting from their shoulders. Unlike their relatives, they did not have bony clubs on their tails. Nodosaurs were usually large, with four pillar-like legs to take their weight.

In 2011, paleontologists were very excited when a fossil of a new nodosaur, now named *Borealopelta* (meaning "northern shield"), was found by miners in Canada. Unlike most fossils, in which the animal's soft skin and flesh has largely rotted away, this dead animal had been buried so quickly by sand that it had kept much of its skin.

The result was a fossil that showed exactly where *Borealopelta's* scutes were positioned, as well as how the scutes were covered in skin and tough horn. Tests on the skin, and the small scales that surrounded the scutes, have shown that *Borealopelta* was reddish-brown, with paler dapples that helped with camouflage.

Even the contents of *Borealopelta's* stomach were preserved, showing that its last meal was almost entirely ferns. This suggests that nodosaurs were selective about the food they ate, reaching for their chosen leaves with their narrow, hard-edged beaks.

Beneath its skin, *Polacanthus's* scutes were often joined together to form large, solid shields that no predator could have pierced.

Family:	Nodosauridae
Range:	North America, Europe, Asia, Africa, and Antarctica
Time Period:	Late Jurassic to late Cretaceous, 155–66 million years ago
Size Range:	3–7 m (9.8–23 ft) long

Acanthopholis

Panoplosaurus

ANKYLOSAURS

The ankylosaurid family had bony clubs on the tips of their tails that could have given enemies a vicious blow. Their bodies and skulls were covered in thick scutes, with tiny scutes filling the gaps between big ones to make an almost solid shield. The last of the ankylosaurs died out after an asteroid careered into Earth 66 million years ago.

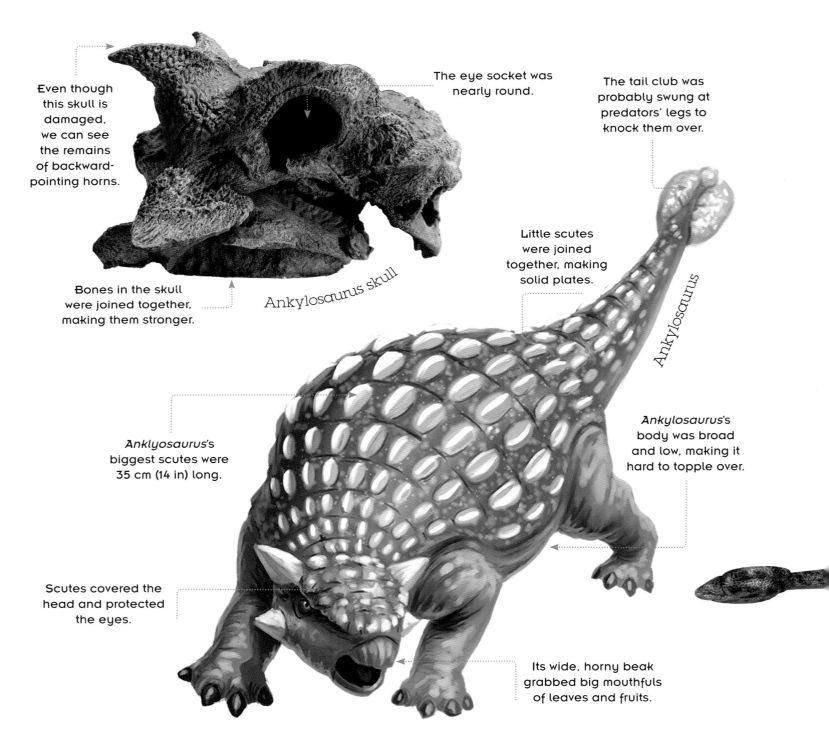

Even though this skull is damaged, we can see the remains of backward-pointing horns.

The eye socket was nearly round.

The tail club was probably swung at predators' legs to knock them over.

Bones in the skull were joined together, making them stronger.

Ankylosaurus skull

Little scutes were joined together, making solid plates.

Ankylosaurus

Anklyosaurus's biggest scutes were 35 cm (14 in) long.

Ankylosaurus's body was broad and low, making it hard to topple over.

Scutes covered the head and protected the eyes.

Its wide, horny beak grabbed big mouthfuls of leaves and fruits.

Family:	Ankylosauridae
Range:	North America, Europe, and Asia
Time Period:	Early Cretaceous to late Cretaceous, 122–66 million years ago
Size Range:	3.6–8 m (11.8–26 ft) long

Shanxia Ankylosaurus

Up to 57 cm (22 in) wide, the club was made of several, joined scutes.

Ankylosaurus tail

These tail bones, called vertebrae, were stuck together to make a stiff rod at the base of the club.

Talarurus means "basket tail," as the tail club looks a little like a woven basket.

Talarurus

The neck was well protected by scutes.

Euoplocephalus

Only the legs were not covered by scutes.

TAKING TO WATER AND SKY

Reptiles walked on all fours on land for around 15 million years after they first evolved. Then, 300 million years ago, some reptiles ventured into oceans and lakes. About 70 million years later, other reptiles jumped, glided, and finally flapped into the sky.

Long before the dinosaurs evolved, some land-living reptiles started to adapt to life in water. Over millions of years, their legs developed into flippers and their bodies grew more smoothly shaped, or streamlined, to help with swimming. Like all reptiles, these swimming reptiles needed to breathe air, so they came regularly to the water surface. Some, such as crocodile-like reptiles, continued to lay eggs on land. Others, including ichthyosaurs, now had bodies so unsuited to land that they gave birth to live, swimming young in the water. While dinosaurs reigned on land, swimming reptiles were top predators in the oceans.

The flying reptiles, called pterosaurs (meaning "wing lizards" in ancient Greek), were cousins of the dinosaurs. To adapt to life in the air, they developed hollow, air-filled bones to make them lightweight. Their arms and hands developed into wings. Although their skin still had patches of scales, they were largely covered in hair-like threads, softer than feathers, called pycnofibers (or picnofibres).

Up to 4.6 m (15 ft) long, *Archelon* was a turtle that swam in the oceans 80 to 74 million years ago. Unlike pterosaurs and dinosaurs, some turtles survived when an asteroid hit Earth 66 million years ago.

On Hateg Island in the Tethys Sea, the 5.5-m (18-ft) tall pterosaur *Hatzegopteryx* attacks a crocodile-like *Acynodon*.

Pterosaur Wings

Pterosaur wings were flaps of skin that stretched from their legs to the extra-long fourth finger of each arm. The other three, clawed fingers stuck out from the front of the wing. The flaps were strengthened by muscles and tough cords. Pterosaurs probably took off by using both arms and legs to make a standing jump into the sky.

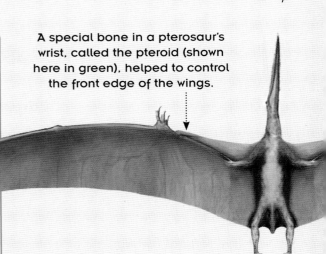

A special bone in a pterosaur's wrist, called the pteroid (shown here in green), helped to control the front edge of the wings.

FLIGHT

Pterosaurs were the earliest backboned animals, called vertebrates, to start to fly. Yet the very first flying animals were insects, which are invertebrates, without a backbone. Of the six animal groups—invertebrates, fish, amphibians, reptiles, mammals, and birds—only some invertebrates, mammals, and birds can fly today.

Around 325 million years ago, grasshoppers and dragonflies were the first known flying animals. They probably evolved the ability to fly as they jumped into the air, or skimmed over water, their little winglets growing larger over time. After a few million years, they could glide, or soar through the air without flapping their wings. Finally, these insects became capable of powered flight: flying by flapping their wings.

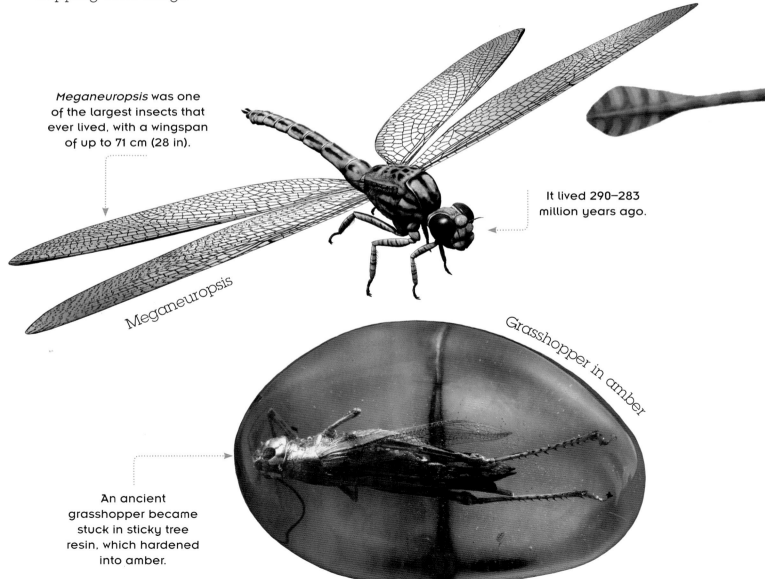

Meganeuropsis was one of the largest insects that ever lived, with a wingspan of up to 71 cm (28 in).

It lived 290–283 million years ago.

Meganeuropsis

Grasshopper in amber

An ancient grasshopper became stuck in sticky tree resin, which hardened into amber.

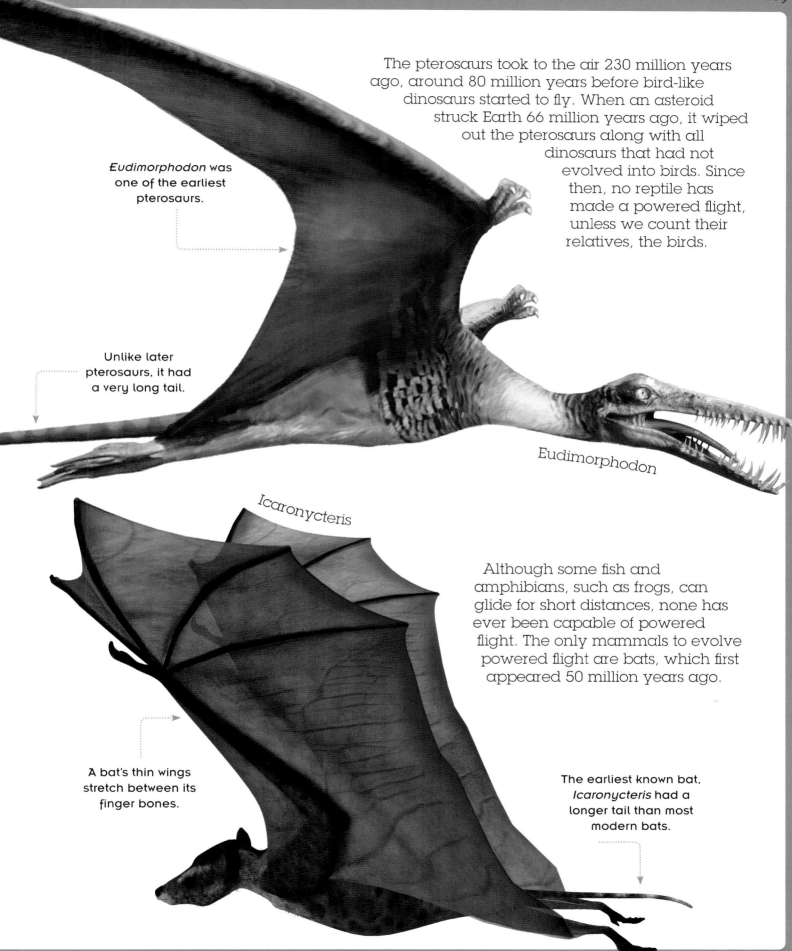

The pterosaurs took to the air 230 million years ago, around 80 million years before bird-like dinosaurs started to fly. When an asteroid struck Earth 66 million years ago, it wiped out the pterosaurs along with all dinosaurs that had not evolved into birds. Since then, no reptile has made a powered flight, unless we count their relatives, the birds.

Eudimorphodon was one of the earliest pterosaurs.

Unlike later pterosaurs, it had a very long tail.

Eudimorphodon

Icaronycteris

Although some fish and amphibians, such as frogs, can glide for short distances, none has ever been capable of powered flight. The only mammals to evolve powered flight are bats, which first appeared 50 million years ago.

A bat's thin wings stretch between its finger bones.

The earliest known bat, *Icaronycteris* had a longer tail than most modern bats.

The fossilized contents of *Rhamphorhynchus* throats and stomachs have revealed the remains of little fish such as *Leptolepides*.

RHAMPHORHYNCHOIDS

These early pterosaurs were usually small, with narrow wings that stretched no more than 2.5 m (8.2 ft) from wingtip to wingtip. They had long, stiff tails that ended in a vane, a flap of skin and body tissue that helped with steering and steadying the rhamphorhynchoid in flight.

Pterosaurs are divided into two main groups, called suborders: the rhamphorhynchoids and the later pterodactyloids. The rhamphorhynchoids are named after *Rhamphorhynchus* (meaning "beak snout" in ancient Greek), which was first found and studied in Germany in 1825.

Rhamphorhynchus's jaws suggest it was a fish-eater. The jaws were long, ending in a sharp beak-like tip with an upcurving hook on the lower jaw. Like the beaks of modern seabirds such as pelicans, this beak would have been ideal for scooping slippery fish. The pterosaur's needle-like teeth interlocked when its mouth was closed, forming a trap that small fish could not have escaped.

Paleontologists think that, unlike modern seabirds such as albatrosses, *Rhamphorhynchus* did

not snatch prey from the water surface. Instead, like modern cormorants, this pterosaur dived beneath the surface, paddling with its broad feet. Its large eyes would have helped *Rhamphorhynchus* see underwater or even to hunt at night. It lived along sea coasts, but may also have dived into rivers and lakes.

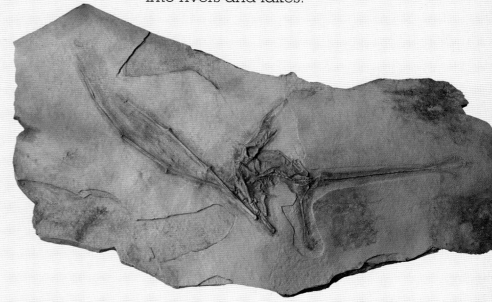

The imprint of *Rhamphorhynchus*'s skin can be seen in this fossil: its wings (on the left) and its tail vane (on the far right).

Suborder:	Rhamphorhynchoidea
Range:	North America, South America, Europe, and Asia
Time Period:	Late Triassic to late Cretaceous, 221–94 million years ago
Size Range:	0.6–1.8 m (2–6 ft) long

Scaphognathus   Harpactognathus

PTERODACTYLOIDS

Pterodactyloids (meaning "finger wings") were descendants of the earlier rhamphorhynchoids. Pterodactyloids had shorter tails than rhamphorhynchoids, but much longer hand bones, giving them very wide wings. Many pterodactyloids had a crest on their head, which may have been displayed when they wanted to attract a mate.

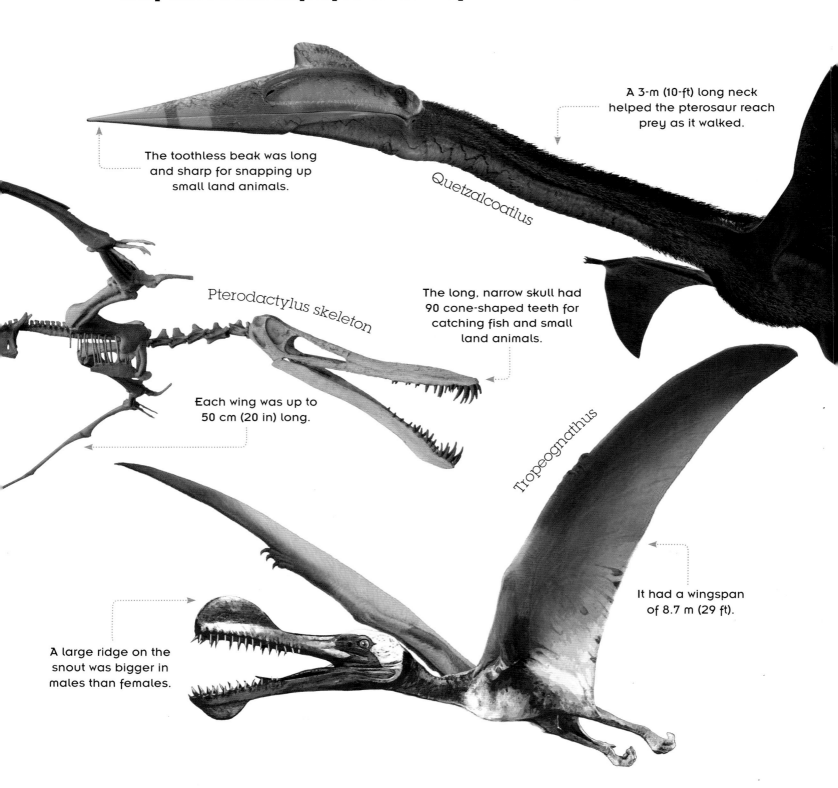

A 3-m (10-ft) long neck helped the pterosaur reach prey as it walked.

The toothless beak was long and sharp for snapping up small land animals.

Quetzalcoatlus

Pterodactylus skeleton

The long, narrow skull had 90 cone-shaped teeth for catching fish and small land animals.

Each wing was up to 50 cm (20 in) long.

Tropeognathus

A large ridge on the snout was bigger in males than females.

It had a wingspan of 8.7 m (29 ft).

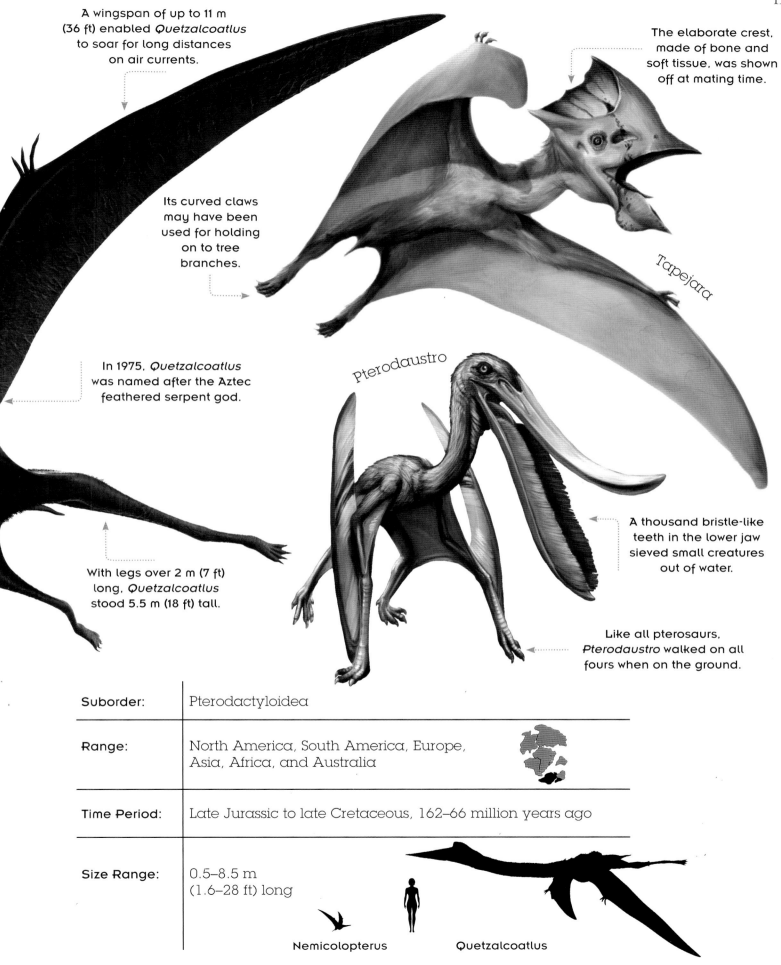

A wingspan of up to 11 m (36 ft) enabled *Quetzalcoatlus* to soar for long distances on air currents.

The elaborate crest, made of bone and soft tissue, was shown off at mating time.

Its curved claws may have been used for holding on to tree branches.

Tapejara

In 1975, *Quetzalcoatlus* was named after the Aztec feathered serpent god.

Pterodaustro

With legs over 2 m (7 ft) long, *Quetzalcoatlus* stood 5.5 m (18 ft) tall.

A thousand bristle-like teeth in the lower jaw sieved small creatures out of water.

Like all pterosaurs, *Pterodaustro* walked on all fours when on the ground.

Suborder:	Pterodactyloidea
Range:	North America, South America, Europe, Asia, Africa, and Australia
Time Period:	Late Jurassic to late Cretaceous, 162–66 million years ago
Size Range:	0.5–8.5 m (1.6–28 ft) long

Nemicolopterus   Quetzalcoatlus

PTERANODONTIDS

The pteranodontids were a family of large pterodactyls with long, bony crests that jutted from the back of their head. Unlike most earlier pterosaurs, their beaks were completely toothless. The pteranodontids were among the last pterosaurs to flap through the skies, before they were wiped out 66 million years ago.

The pteranodontid family was named after the *Pteranodon* (meaning "toothless wing") species, of which more than 1,200 fossils have been found in North America. *Pteranodon*'s curved toothless beak was similar to a bird's, with bony edges that stuck up from the jaw bones. This beak was used for snapping up fish or squid while *Pteranodon* dived in shallow inland seas. The location of its fossils suggests that *Pteranodon* came to land on small islands, where it could lay eggs away from most of its predators.

Fully grown male pteranodontids had much longer crests than females and young males, which had rounder crests. Among modern animals, when males have larger body features than females, they often use them for attracting females or driving other males away from their territory. This is how male deer use their

antlers. Paleontologists think that male pteranodontids showed off their crests to females by dancing or strutting. Males with big crests may have driven away smaller-crested males from the rocky islands where they mated.

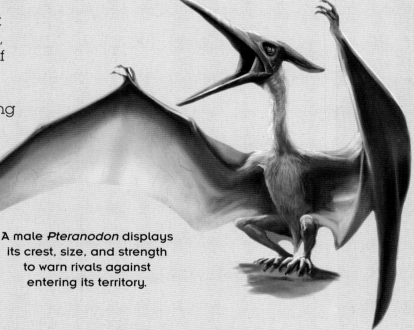

A male *Pteranodon* displays its crest, size, and strength to warn rivals against entering its territory.

Family:	Pteranodontidae
Range:	Seas of North America, Asia, and Africa
Time Period:	Late Cretaceous, 88–66 million years ago
Size Range:	2.5–2.8 m (8.2–9.2 ft) long

Tethydraco   Pteranodon

A flock of *Tethydraco* nests on an island in Cretaceous North Africa.

ICHTHYOSAURS

Ichthyosaurs (meaning "fish lizards") were the oceans' most deadly predators for many millions of years, before they faced competition from the arrival of the plesiosaurs. Most ichthyosaurs had cone-shaped teeth for gripping fish, but larger species had knife-like teeth for ripping any smaller creature that came their way.

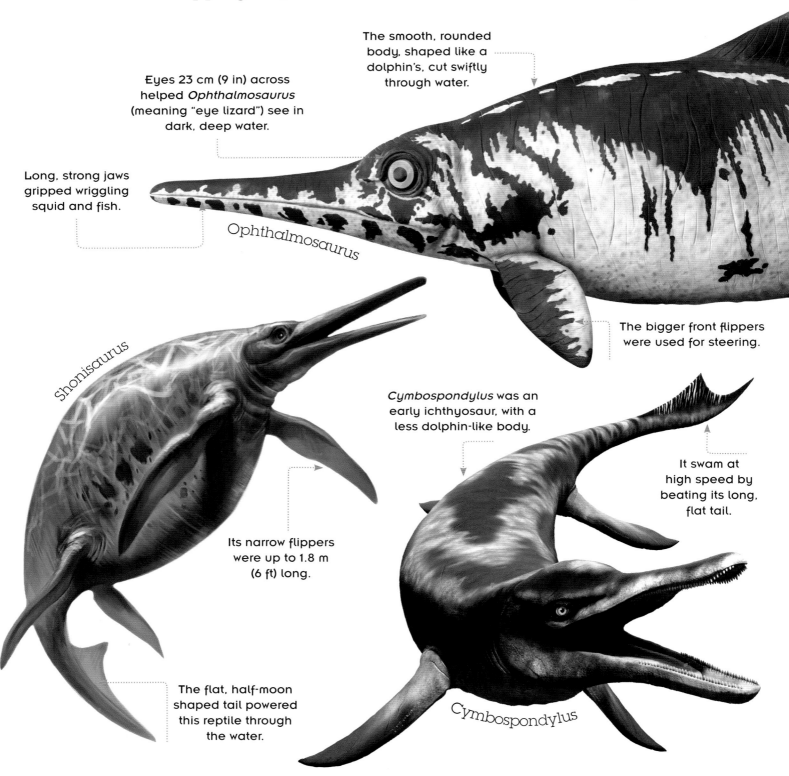

The smooth, rounded body, shaped like a dolphin's, cut swiftly through water.

Eyes 23 cm (9 in) across helped *Ophthalmosaurus* (meaning "eye lizard") see in dark, deep water.

Long, strong jaws gripped wriggling squid and fish.

Ophthalmosaurus

Shonisaurus

The bigger front flippers were used for steering.

Cymbospondylus was an early ichthyosaur, with a less dolphin-like body.

It swam at high speed by beating its long, flat tail.

Its narrow flippers were up to 1.8 m (6 ft) long.

The flat, half-moon shaped tail powered this reptile through the water.

Cymbospondylus

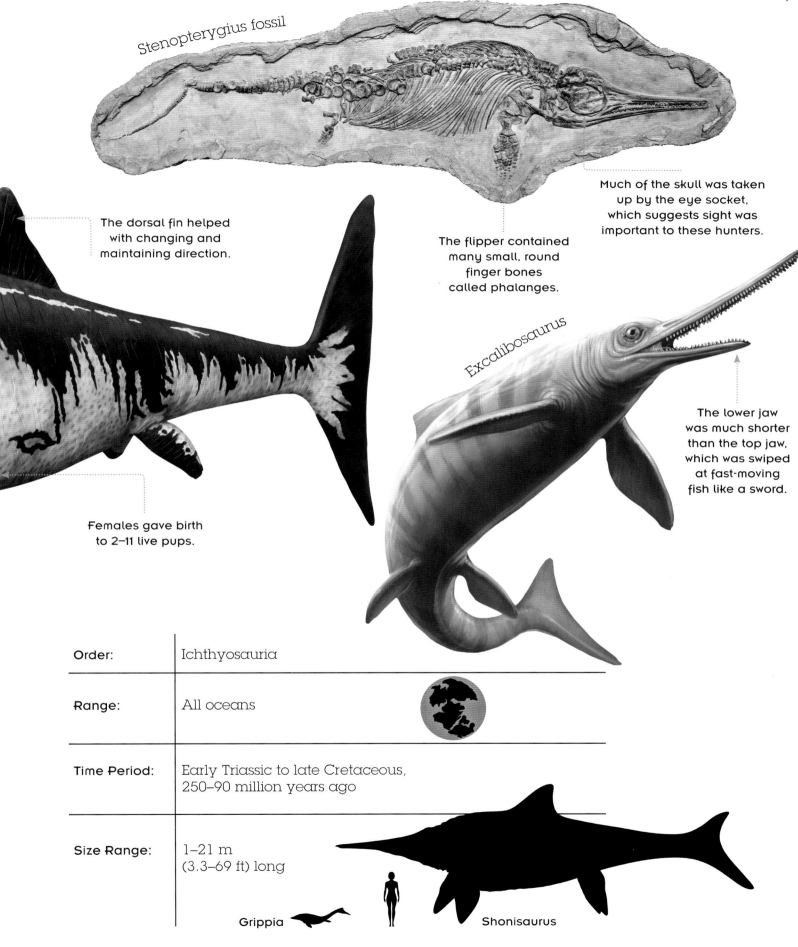

Stenopterygius fossil

The dorsal fin helped with changing and maintaining direction.

Much of the skull was taken up by the eye socket, which suggests sight was important to these hunters.

The flipper contained many small, round finger bones called phalanges.

Excalibosaurus

The lower jaw was much shorter than the top jaw, which was swiped at fast-moving fish like a sword.

Females gave birth to 2–11 live pups.

Order:	Ichthyosauria
Range:	All oceans
Time Period:	Early Triassic to late Cretaceous, 250–90 million years ago
Size Range:	1–21 m (3.3–69 ft) long

Grippia

Shonisaurus

PLESIOSAURS

These ocean-dwelling reptiles usually had very long necks.
These necks helped with feeding, perhaps by scooping along
the seafloor or by surprising shoals of fish. Plesiosaur
teeth were suited to capturing prey but not to chewing.
Plesiosaurs swallowed small creatures whole, along with
occasional pebbles to grind up food inside the stomach.

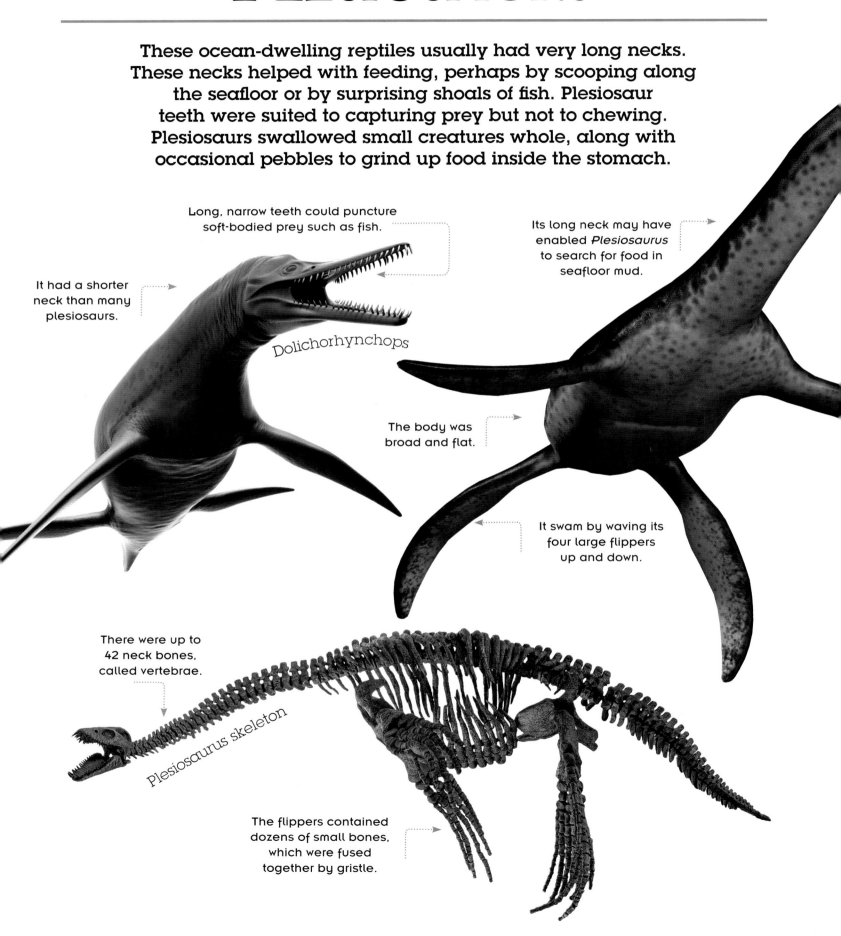

Long, narrow teeth could puncture
soft-bodied prey such as fish.

Its long neck may have
enabled *Plesiosaurus*
to search for food in
seafloor mud.

It had a shorter
neck than many
plesiosaurs.

Dolichorhynchops

The body was
broad and flat.

It swam by waving its
four large flippers
up and down.

There were up to
42 neck bones,
called vertebrae.

Plesiosaurus skeleton

The flippers contained
dozens of small bones,
which were fused
together by gristle.

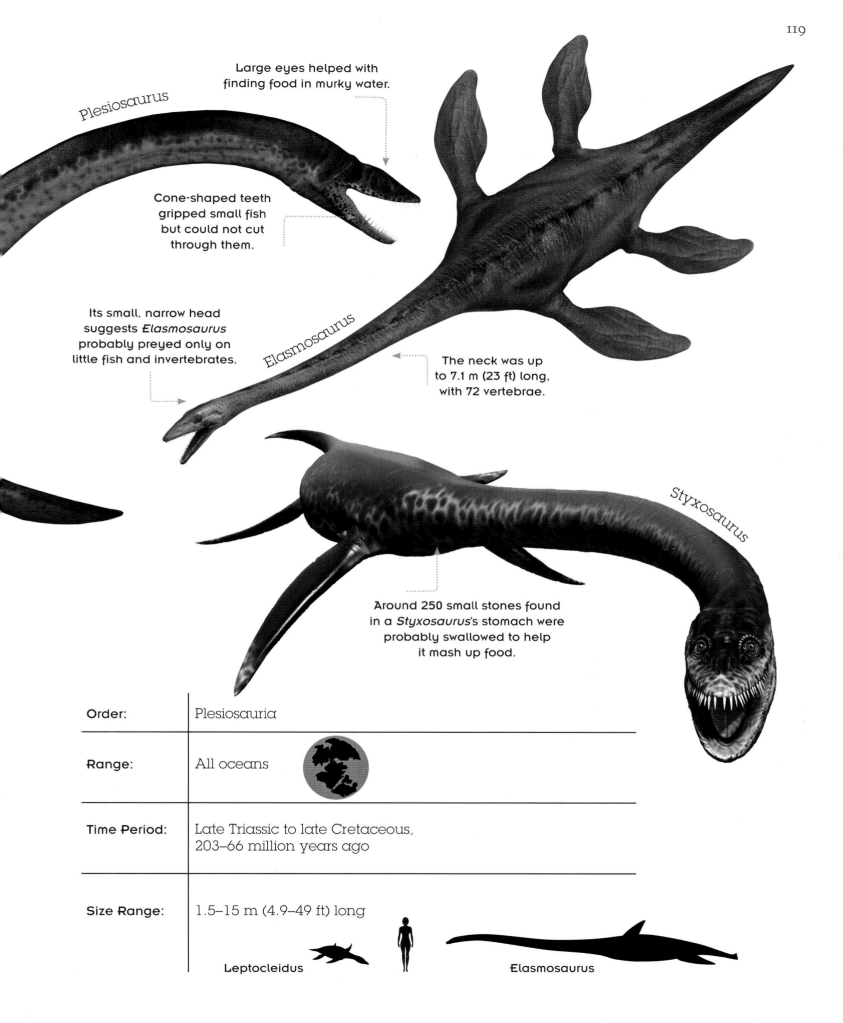

Plesiosaurus

Large eyes helped with finding food in murky water.

Cone-shaped teeth gripped small fish but could not cut through them.

Its small, narrow head suggests _Elasmosaurus_ probably preyed only on little fish and invertebrates.

Elasmosaurus

The neck was up to 7.1 m (23 ft) long, with 72 vertebrae.

Styxosaurus

Around 250 small stones found in a _Styxosaurus_'s stomach were probably swallowed to help it mash up food.

Order:	Plesiosauria
Range:	All oceans
Time Period:	Late Triassic to late Cretaceous, 203–66 million years ago
Size Range:	1.5–15 m (4.9–49 ft) long

Leptocleidus

Elasmosaurus

In the Eromanga Sea of Cretaceous Australia,
Kronosaurus grasps the unprotected neck
of an *Eromangasaurus*.

PLIOSAURS

The pliosaurs were a family of short-necked plesiosaurs with large heads. Far fiercer than their relatives, they had long, crocodile-like jaws lined with sharp teeth. Strong jaw bones and muscles gave them powerful bites, able to crush the bodies of other swimming reptiles, such as plesiosaurs and turtles, as well as fish and squid.

Large pliosaurs, such as *Kronosaurus*, *Liopleurodon*, and *Pliosaurus*, were among the deadliest marine reptiles that ever lived. Powered by their four broad flippers, they could reach speeds of 10 km (6 miles) per hour, about as fast as the best human swimmers. Their large, muscly bodies weighed up to 12 tonnes (13 US tons), more than six cars. Pliosaur mothers probably gave birth to just one or two fully formed babies, already at least 1.5 m (4.9 ft) long.

Kronosaurus had rows of cone-shaped teeth up to 30 cm (12 in) long. Unlike those of deadly sharks, these teeth did not have sharp cutting edges. However, *Kronosaurus* could have gripped its prey hard enough to crush or shake it to death. *Kronosaurus* tooth marks have been found on other marine reptiles, including the 10-m (33-ft) long plesiosaur *Eromangasaurus*.

Long before the widespread extinctions of 66 million years ago, the pliosaurs had disappeared. They were probably driven to extinction by even larger and sharper-toothed marine predators, such as mosasaurs and megatoothed sharks, which reached 18 m (59 ft) long.

Family:	Pliosauridae
Range:	All oceans
Time Period:	Late Triassic to late Cretaceous, 228–89 million years ago
Size Range:	1.5–10.9 m (4.9–36 ft) long

Thalassiodracon   Kronosaurus

Liopleurodon probably had a good sense of smell, able to sense prey long before it came into view.

MOSASAURS

Most mosasaurs were large, fast-swimming predators with immensely strong jaws. The biggest mosasaurs were at the top of their ocean food chain, with no animals large enough to prey on them. Mosasaurs were named after the Meuse River in the Netherlands, where fossils of these reptiles were first found and studied, in 1764.

Mosasaurs had streamlined bodies, able to move smoothly through the water. They swam by beating their large tails. Like some modern sharks, they probably moved slowly toward prey, saving a burst of speed for the last moment. Most mosasaurs were big enough to prey on whatever animals they came across, from plesiosaurs to birds and fish. Their eyes were large, suggesting they relied on sight to find prey.

Mosasaurs' heavily muscled jaws had dozens of teeth with blade-like edges. They had an extra row of teeth at the back of their upper jaw, inside the main teeth, which helped them hold onto prey as they swallowed it. Their bottom jaw could be moved back and forward, as well as opening and closing, which enabled mosasaur jaws to snap shut on prey with deadly force.

The sea level was high during the warm Cretaceous Period, because water expands when it gets hotter. This meant that oceans flooded many inland areas of the world's continents. A wide range of mosasaur fossils have been found in these shallow inland seas.

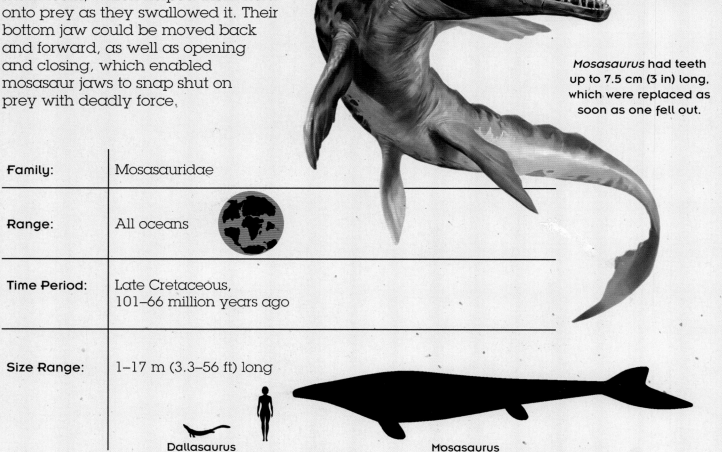

Mosasaurus had teeth up to 7.5 cm (3 in) long, which were replaced as soon as one fell out.

Family:	Mosasauridae
Range:	All oceans
Time Period:	Late Cretaceous, 101–66 million years ago
Size Range:	1–17 m (3.3–56 ft) long

Dallasaurus

Mosasaurus

Reaching 14 m (46 ft) long, *Tylosaurus* tries to snap up the shark *Hybodus*.

CROCODILES

Around 250 million years ago, a group of crocodile-like reptiles, called pseudosuchians, evolved. One group of pseudosuchians, the crocodylomorphs, survived the catastrophe of 66 million years ago. More than 20 species of crocodylomorphs are alive today, in four groups: the crocodiles, alligators, caimans, and gharials.

Most pseudosuchians, past and present, have a large skull with a long, narrow snout. Their body is often protected by rows of thick plates, called scutes. Before dinosaurs evolved, pseudosuchians were very successful on land. Some were fierce, giant predators, but others were small and slim, eating shellfish, insects, or plants.

From 230 to 203 million years ago, 5-m (16-ft) long *Postosuchus* was one of the largest land predators in North America.

Postosuchus

It may have walked on its long back legs.

Desmatosuchus

This plant-eating pseudosuchian lived 228–210 million years ago.

From around 200 million years ago, the crocodylomorphs developed more crocodile-like bodies. Some were still land-living, while others spent all their time in water. Some, like today's crocodiles, spent part of their life in water and part on land. Although dinosaurs were now the top predators on land, a wide range of crocodylomorphs ruled the swamps, rivers, and oceans. Today, the descendants of those crocodylomorphs are the closest living relatives of birds.

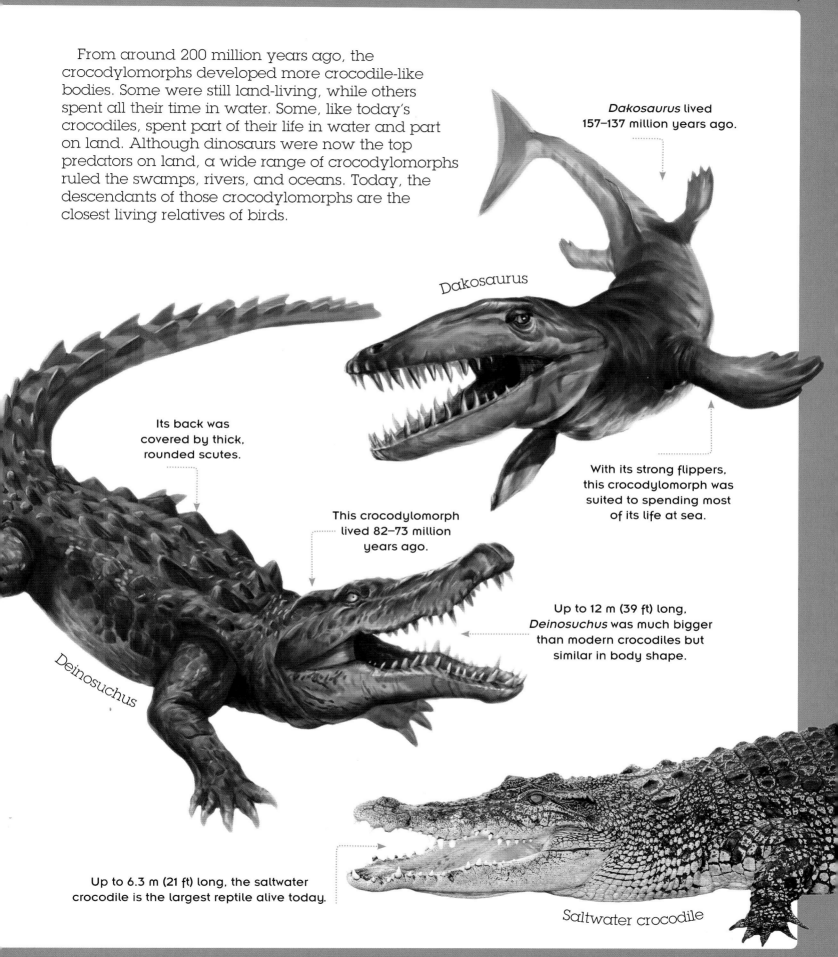

Dakosaurus lived 157–137 million years ago.

Dakosaurus

Its back was covered by thick, rounded scutes.

This crocodylomorph lived 82–73 million years ago.

With its strong flippers, this crocodylomorph was suited to spending most of its life at sea.

Deinosuchus

Up to 12 m (39 ft) long, *Deinosuchus* was much bigger than modern crocodiles but similar in body shape.

Up to 6.3 m (21 ft) long, the saltwater crocodile is the largest reptile alive today.

Saltwater crocodile

GLOSSARY

AMPHIBIAN An animal that usually spends part of its life in water and part on land.

ARCHOSAUR An animal belonging to a group of vertebrates that includes dinosaurs, birds, pterosaurs, and crocodiles.

BIRD An animal with feathers, wings, and a beak, descended from theropod dinosaurs.

CELL The smallest working part of a living thing.

CERAPOD An ornithischian, plant-eating dinosaur with a beak and ridged teeth.

CERATOPSIAN A cerapod dinosaur that often had horns and neck frills.

CRETACEOUS PERIOD A period of Earth's history lasting from 145 to 66 million years ago.

DINOSAUR An extinct, land-living reptile that walked with its back legs held directly beneath its body.

EVOLUTION The slow process of change and development in living things.

FAMILY A group of closely related species.

FOSSIL The preserved remains of an animal or plant that lived in the distant past.

INVERTEBRATE An animal without a backbone, such as an insect or jellyfish.

JURASSIC PERIOD A period of Earth's history lasting from 201 to 145 million years ago.

MAMMAL An animal that grows hair and feeds its babies on milk.

MICRO-ORGANISM A simple, tiny living thing.

MINERAL A solid, natural substance.

ORNITHISCHIAN A plant-eating dinosaur with hips similar to those of birds.

PACHYCEPHALOSAUR A cerapod dinosaur with a thick, often domed, skull.

PALEONTOLOGY The study of fossils.

PREY An animal that is hunted for food.

PTEROSAUR An extinct reptile with wings attached to its extra-long fourth fingers.

REPTILE An animal with lungs that usually has scaly skin and lays eggs on land.

SAURISCHIAN A dinosaur with hips similar to those of lizards.

SAUROPODOMORPH A plant-eating saurischian dinosaur with a long neck.

SCALE A small, hard plate that grows from an animal's skin for protection.

SCUTE A bony plate with a horny covering.

SPECIES A group of living things that look similar and can make babies together.

TETRAPOD An animal with four limbs, or with four-limbed ancestors, such as an amphibian, reptile, bird, or mammal.

THEROPOD A saurischian dinosaur with hollow bones and, usually, three main toes.

THYREOPHORAN An ornithischian, plant-eating dinosaur with scutes for protection.

TRIASSIC PERIOD A period of Earth's history lasting from 252 to 201 million years ago.

VERTEBRATE An animal with a backbone, such as a fish, amphibian, reptile, bird, or mammal.

PRONUNCIATION GUIDE

ALLOSAURUS AL-oh-SORE-us

AMARGASAURUS ah-MARG-ah-SORE-us

ANCHIORNIS AN-kee-OR-niss

ANKYLOSAURUS an-KIH-loh-SORE-us

ARCHAEOPTERYX ARK-ee-OPT-er-ix

ARGENTINOSAURUS AR-juhn-TEE-no-SORE-us

BARYONYX BAH-ree-ON-icks

BRACHIOSAURUS BRAH-kee-oh-SORE-us

CARNOTAURUS KAR-no-TORE-us

CAUDIPTERYX CAW-DIP-the-rix

CENTROSAURUS SEN-tro-SORE-us

CERATOSAURUS keh-RAT-oh-SORE-us

CHASMOSAURUS KAZ-moh-SORE-us

COELOPHYSIS see-loh-FISE-iss

COMPSOGNATHUS komp-sog-NAY-thus

DEINONYCHUS dy-NON-ik-us

DEINOSUCHUS dy-no-SOO-kus

DILOPHOSAURUS dy-LOFF-oh-SORE-us

DIPLODOCUS dip-LOH-doh-kus

DYMORPHODON dy-MOR-foh-don

ELASMOSAURUS el-LAZZ-moh-SORE-us

EORAPTOR EE-oh-RAP-tuhr

EUOPLOCEPHALUS you-OH-plo-KEF-ah-lus

GALLIMIMUS gal-uh-MY-mus

GASTONIA gas-TOH-nee-ah

GIGANOTOSAURUS jig-an-OH-toe-SORE-us

HADROSAURUS HAD-ro-SORE-us

HETERODONTOSAURUS HET-er-oh-DONT-oh-SORE-us

ICHTHYOSAURUS ICK-thee-oh-SORE-us

IGUANODON ig-WAH-noh-don

LESOTHOSAURUS leh-SOO-too-SORE-us

LILIENSTERNUS LIL-ee-en-SHTURN-us

LIOPLEURODON LY-oh-PLOO-ro-don

MAIASAURA MY-ah-SORE-ah

MAMENCHISAURUS MAH-men-kee-SORE-us

MEGALODON meh-GAH-lo-don

MICRORAPTOR MY-kroh-rap-tuhr

MOSASAURUS MOH-sah-SORE-us

NODOSAURUS NOH-doh-SORE-us

PACHYCEPHALOSAURUS pak-ee-SEF-ah-lo-SORE-us

PARASAUROLOPHUS PA-ra-sore-OL-off-us

PLATEOSAURUS PLAT-ee-oh-SORE-us

PLESIOSAURUS PLEH-zee-oh-SORE-us

POSTOSUCHUS POST-oh-SOOK-us

PROTOCERATOPS PRO-toh-SEH-rah-tops

PSITTACOSAURUS SIT-ak-oh-SORE-us

PTERANODON teh-RAH-no-don

PTERODACTYLUS TEH-ro-DACK-tih-lus

PTEROSAUR TEH-roh-sore

QUETZALCOATLUS KWETS-ul-koh-AT-lus

RHAMPHORHYNCHUS RAM-foh-RINK-us

SCELIDOSAURUS SKEL-id-oh-SORE-us

SCUTELLOSAURUS skoo-TELL-oh-SORE-us

SHONISAURUS SHON-ee-SORE-us

SINOSAUROPTERYX SIGH-no-sore-OP-tuh-rix

SPINOSAURUS SPINE-oh-SORE-us

STEGOSAURUS STEG-oh-SORE-us

STYRACOSAURUS sty-RACK-oh-SORE-us

SUCHOMIMUS SOOK-oh-mim-us

TARBOSAURUS TAR-boh-SORE-us

THERIZONOSAURUS THEH-rih-ZIN-oh-sore-us

TITANOBOA ty-TAN-oh-BO-ah

TOROSAURUS TOR-oh-SORE-us

TRICERATOPS try-SEH-ra-tops

TROODON TROH-oh-don

TROPEOGNATHUS TRO-pee-og-NAY-thus

TYRANNOSAURUS REX ty-RAN-oh-SORE-us REX

VELOCIRAPTOR veh-LOSS-ee-rap-tuhr

INDEX